25
TOUGH
QUESTIONS
ABOUT
Women
AND Church
THE

J. LEE GRADY

Charisma
HOUSE
A STRANG COMPANY

25 TOUGH QUESTIONS ABOUT WOMEN AND THE CHURCH by J. Lee Grady
Published by Charisma House
A Strang Company
600 Rinehart Road
Lake Mary, Florida 32746
www.charismahouse.com

Unless otherwise noted, all Scripture quotations are from the New American Standard Bible. Copyright © 1960, 1962, 1963, 1968, 1971, 1972, 1973, 1975, 1977 by the Lockman Foundation. Used by permission. (www.Lockman.org)

Scripture quotations marked KJV are from the King James Version of the Bible.

Scripture quotations marked NIV are from the Holy Bible, New International Version. Copyright © 1973, 1978, 1984, International Bible Society. Used by permission.

Scripture quotations marked NKJV are from the New King James Version of the Bible. Copyright © 1979, 1980, 1982 by Thomas Nelson, Inc., publishers. Used by permission.

Scripture quotations marked NRSV are from the New Revised Standard Version of the Bible. Copyright © 1989 by the Division of Christian Education of the National Council of the Churches of Christ in the USA. Used by permission.

Cover design by Judith McKittrick
Typography by Sallie Traynor

Library of Congress Cataloging-in-Publication Data:
Grady, J. Lee.
  25 tough questions about women and the church / J. Lee Grady.
     p. cm.
Includes bibliographical references.
  ISBN 0-88419-955-X (pbk.)
  1. Women in church work. 2. Women--Religious aspects--Christianity.
3. Feminism--Religious aspects--Christianity. I. Title: Twenty five tough questions about women and the church. II. Title.
  BV639.W7G72 2003
  261.8'344--dc21

                    2003004728

        06 07 08 09 10— 9876543
        Printed in the United States of America

To Gloria Madugba, Abiola Olufeyinmi,
Christy Jireh, Laide Okafor, Nkoyo Rapu and all
the other brave Christian women of Nigeria who
are blazing trails for the gospel.

Contents

The church, in so many ways, is a sort of potter's field where the gifts of women, as so many strangers, are buried. How long, O Lord, how long before man shall roll away the stone that we may see a resurrection?[1]

—PHOEBE PALMER (1807–1874)
AMERICAN PREACHER AND SOCIAL REFORMER

Introduction

The woman who wrote the words on the previous page died more than a generation before women in the United States won the right to vote. Yet this fearless preacher of holiness led at least twenty-five thousand people to Christ during her years of ministry, and she also worked tirelessly to help the poor and disadvantaged. She led campaigns for prison reform, aided destitute women and founded a relief mission in one of New York City's worst slums. Yet despite her good works, the door of opportunity was often slammed in her face when she stood to preach.

Church leaders in the 1840s and 1850s believed that women should be silent in the church. Using one passage from the apostle Paul's first letter to the Corinthians as an unbendable mandate for all time, they expected women to remain passive and invisible. Yet a fire burned in Phoebe Palmer's spirit—a fire she believed had been kindled by the Holy Ghost. She dared not quench it.

There were a few men in Mrs. Palmer's day who recognized that the fire of the Holy Spirit's anointing did indeed burn in the hearts of women, and these men risked their reputations by giving women opportunities to minister publicly. The great American revivalist Charles Finney, in fact, defied the religious traditions of his day when he defended Palmer's right to address large church meetings, even when men were in the audience.

When asked to defend her right to preach, Palmer eloquently explained that Paul's words in 1 Corinthians 14:34—"let the women keep silent"—were not to be applied to all women in all generations. "The apostle," Palmer explained, "was correcting a specific problem in a specific church in a specific time in history. To apply his words to women today," she said, "would be a serious error." Palmer wrote:

> Surely it is evident that the irregularities here com-
> plained of [1 Corinthians 14] were peculiar to the
> church of Corinth, and, in fact, we may presume, were
> not even applicable to other Christian churches of
> Paul's day, much less Christian churches of the present
> day...O, the endless weight of responsibility with which
> the church is pressing herself earthward through the
> depressing influences of this error: How can she rise
> while the gifts of three-fourths of her membership are
> sepulchered in her midst?[2]

Palmer penned those words more than one hundred fifty years
ago. Yet today, much remains the same. Although women in the
United States have civil freedom, equal rights in the workplace and
the full protection of law, many church leaders continue to quench
the fire that burns in our sisters. We deny them equal rights to participate in the life of the church, and we slam the door on opportunities for leadership. We encourage them to be passive, as if
timidity were a virtue. We tell women who believe God has given
them gifts of leadership, prophecy, pastoring or preaching that they
are mistaken and misguided.

Meanwhile, around the world, women remain in serious spiritual and cultural bondage. Those who live in Buddhist, Hindu or
Islamic nations suffer untold cruelty and have no civil right to
educational opportunities. In Latin America, the problem of wife-
beating and sexual abuse of girls is rampant, yet the church seems
powerless to protect women because its misguided theology actually encourages abuse. In Africa, a male-dominated church has not
been willing to bring the reforms necessary to win basic legal
protection for widows and battered women. These problems will
never be solved until men in the church repent of gender prejudice and release women to fulfill their God-given callings.

Introduction

Before you read this book, let me make it clear that I am a radical proponent of equality for women. *25 Tough Questions About Women and the Church* is not a "safe" Christian book that tells women to sit quietly and obediently in the back of the church. We don't need any more of those books. My sisters in Christ have been told for too long to shut up and take a back seat. It is time for a reformation.

I believe we need more women preachers, more women missionaries and, yes, more women pastors. We also need more women reformers to lift up their voices against the tide of evil that threatens to engulf us in this hour—and that means that more Christian women must bring their godly influence into business and government. Because my wife and I have four daughters of our own, defending women comes naturally to me. And I will not be satisfied until the church adopts a radically different paradigm that allows women equal opportunity based not on gender but on Spirit-anointed giftings.

Since my first book on this subject, *10 Lies the Church Tells Women,* was published in 2000, I have been called many names: "Christian feminist," "egalitarian," "liberal" and "heretic." The names don't bother me because I always knew I would be opposed if I stuck my neck out to defend my sisters. But I can assure you that I am not twisting the Bible to prove my point. I believe 100 percent in the inerrancy of Scripture, and I do not have a "liberal" theological agenda. I do believe, however, that conservative, evangelical Christians—with whom I fully identify—often interpret the Bible through the lens of their own ignorance and prejudice rather than by the inspiration of the Holy Spirit. And that is why we so desperately need the Holy Spirit's guidance as we study the Scriptures that deal with women and gender issues. As Bible teacher Fuchsia Pickett often says, we must stop reading our prejudices *into* the Bible and start reading what the Spirit is saying in the text.

Since *10 Lies the Church Tells Women* was released, I have addressed dozens of women's conferences, challenged church leaders to reconsider their views on the subject and even taken my message to Africa and Latin America. The response has been encouraging, even though one major Christian bookstore chain refuses to sell the book because of a denominational policy that restricts women from being in pastoral positions.

Being shut out of a bookstore is one thing. (That actually has helped me identify with some of the rejection women experience every day.) What is more disturbing are the letters I have received from women who feel they have been beaten up—literally and figuratively—by their Christian husbands, pastors and church leaders. I had no idea that physical abuse was so common in Christian marriages until I began to hear from the victims. Sadly, many of these battered women had to go outside the church to find emotional and psychological help because so few pastors are equipped to address the issue. Often, women are simply told to "submit" when they are enduring physical cruelty in their marriages. Some of them end up in the hospital as a result. And I know of one woman who was murdered because she obediently submitted to the blows of a husband who sat on the deacon board of his church.

Women have also endured incredible injustice when it comes to exclusion from ministry opportunities. Evangelical seminaries take money from women and train them, but then the very institutions they support often deny them a place to minister. Denominations say one thing and do another when it comes to giving women positions of authority. Pastors tell single women they cannot have a position in the church until they have a Christian husband to "cover" them, even though the same standard is not applied to single men. And thousands of women who feel called to work for the Lord in some capacity are hamstrung because their Christian husbands, for whatever reason, object.

This book was written as a response to the many questions I have received from women after they read my first book or heard me speak at a conference. I've tried to write these answers as simply and plainly as possible, knowing that entire books have been written on many of the questions addressed here. I offer it as a comprehensive guide to help address the many issues women face, either in marriage or in ministry. I pray that this book will help bring these questions out in the open. We've swept them under the rug long enough.

It is rather pitiful that we are still asking these questions in the twenty-first century. The Holy Spirit has used women in powerful ways since the Day of Pentecost—from the brave women martyrs of the first century to today's growing army of female church-planters in China. Yet men have always found a way to erect barriers, draw lines and place restrictions on women. We have misinterpreted and mistranslated verses in the Bible to bolster our own prejudices, and—out of ignorance and bondage to religious mind-sets—we have told our sisters that their gender disqualifies them from full participation.

Meanwhile, in the home, Christian women have been told that God expects them to live in a state of subjection, as if they were secondary supporters rather than equal partners in marriage. While Scripture clearly tells us that husbands and wives should enjoy a relationship of mutuality, intimacy and partnership, we often teach men that it is acceptable for them to view their husbandly role as dominant and superior. This pagan, hierarchical view of marriage has resulted in a skyrocketing divorce rate among Bible-believing Christians, as well as a growing problem with domestic abuse that

Christian leaders don't like to talk about.

The apostle Paul, who had women such as Priscilla, Phoebe, Euodia and Syntyche on his traveling apostolic team, challenged the church in Galatia to break free from religious and legalistic mind-sets. Even though the Galatian Christians had received an unadulterated message of grace, they had been "bewitched" by the spirit of religion (Gal. 3:1). It is interesting that it was to this church, which had become paralyzed by the traditions and doctrines of men, that Paul wrote his most famous words about the gender issue.

> There is neither Jew nor Greek, slave nor free, male
> nor female, for you are all one in Christ Jesus.
> —GALATIANS 3:28, NIV

Paul's words were a sort of Declaration of Independence, a decree of liberation for all who would be excluded from the life of the church by religious-minded Pharisees. In fact, some scholars call Galatians 3:28 "The Magna Carta of Humanity."[3] In this verse, Paul announced that the church would not be an all-white boys' club, controlled by wealthy patriarchal forces. No—God recognizes no one by skin color, economic class or gender. The Holy Spirit's gifts and ministry callings are distributed freely, as the Spirit determines. (See 1 Corinthians 12:11.)

Paul's words couldn't be clearer. Galatians 3:28 destroys racism, classism and gender prejudice. Yet still today there are religious voices that seek to reinterpret what Paul said plainly. They claim to be biblical literalists, yet they treat this passage cavalierly by explaining it away.

It is in the spirit of Galatians 3:28 that I offer this book. I pray that in my lifetime the body of Christ will throw off the restraints of carnal religious thinking so that we can discover how much

Introduction

God will do through us when we allow the Holy Spirit to have full control of His people. I am anxious to see what will happen when Phoebe Palmer's dream becomes a reality—and the buried spiritual gifts of my sisters are awakened and reactivated for the benefit of Christ's kingdom.

Question #1
Forgiving the Men in Your Life

I've experienced emotional, sexual and even physical abuse from men in my past, and I struggle with anger and unforgiveness toward men as a result. Is there a way to find total freedom from the resentment I feel?

As I have traveled around the country speaking at conferences on the subject of domestic abuse and related topics, I have been appalled at the level of cruelty that is occurring in Christian homes. In 2001 I spoke at a men's event on the subject of "How to Break Free From Male Pride." When I made my final point, I asked the guys in the audience to bow their heads. Then I asked those men to stand who were willing to admit that they were currently involved in some form of physical abuse aimed at their wives.

"When I say physical abuse, I am not just talking about cruel words or angry shouting," I told the men, all of whom were professing born-again believers and active churchgoers. "I am talking about hitting your wives, throwing objects at them, shoving them against a wall or some other form of physical cruelty." Then I asked the men to stand.

It got very quiet in the room. This was a moment of truth. I wondered if pride or fear of exposure would prevent these guys from becoming transparent about a sin that is so embarrassing. But to my amazement, more than twenty men stood in a room of about one hundred fifty. And that number only represented those who were willing to admit their problem.

It was thrilling to watch these men stand with their arms raised to heaven, some of them choking back tears as they humbled themselves before God. For many of them it was the first time they had ever admitted to anyone that they struggled with this unmentionable habit. Finally, when their ugly sin was confronted and brought into the light of God's presence, they found the grace to repent and obtain deliverance from a life-controlling problem.

A few months later I addressed a similarly sized gathering of women on the same subject. At the end of my message, I asked the women to approach the altar if their husbands were beating them or subjecting them to any other form of physical cruelty. At least one-fourth of the women in the room came to the stage, many of them sobbing uncontrollably. Another huge group joined them at the altar when I asked for those who were experiencing emotional cruelty in their marriages.

Let's face it: There is an epidemic of domestic abuse spreading through the church, and most Christian leaders are not addressing this problem. It is usually swept under the rug because pastors feel helplessly untrained in how to counsel abusers (or, in some tragic cases, because the pastors themselves are abusing their wives). And sadly, in some instances, pastors actually use Bible verses about wifely submission to fuel this epidemic of abuse.

According to Dr. John Kie Vining, a Tennessee-based expert in trauma counseling, a woman in the United States is beaten every 7.4 seconds. Domestic abuse is the single greatest cause of injury to women in this country, happening more often than rapes, auto accidents and muggings.[1]

When I spoke at a women's conference in Mexico in late 2002, I learned how serious domestic violence is in Latin American countries where *machismo,* or male dominance, is the cultural norm. Some of the women in my meetings were physically stooped over because their husbands regularly beat them into submission. They had very little self-esteem left. Some of them were living in a prison of depression. Others entertained thoughts of suicide because they saw no hope for escape from the violence they endured in their own homes. Some had developed physical illnesses due to the stress caused by chronic abuse.

One pastor's wife—whose husband had once been physically abusive to her but had repented and found deliverance from this behavior—told me how prevalent domestic violence is in ministers' homes in Mexico. "It is not uncommon for me to receive a call from the hospital—from a pastor's wife," she told me. "She is there because her husband has beaten her. But no one in their church knows about what goes on in their home."

I was shocked when I gave my first altar call at the conference in Mexico. I felt overwhelmed when more than a hundred women rushed to the front of the auditorium to receive prayer for healing from the effects of domestic and cultural abuse. When I prayed for them, I would often begin to sob, as if I were feeling some of their pain. It was almost too much to bear. In broken Spanish I prayed for them: *"Rompo el poder de la oprecion en el nombre de Jesus!"* ("I break the power of oppression in the name of Jesus!")

I also gathered a group of men at the altar, and we knelt on the stage in front of the women. Several of us then repented to the Lord, in front of our sisters, for the way men have treated women—both in our homes and in our churches. We prayed:

Father, we have looked down on the women and treated them like second-class citizens. We have expected them to serve us, bear our children and take care of our homes, but we have not honored them, respected their personal worth or treated them as the precious gifts that they are to us. Forgive us, Lord, for all the verbal cruelty, the physical abuse, the harsh demands, the ungodly domination and the prideful attitudes that have wounded them so deeply.

The Mexican women wailed as they watched these men repent publicly. Many of them could not believe their eyes, because they had never once seen a man repent openly for anything—much less for cruelty to women. A powerful wave of healing was released to the crowd as the men humbled themselves. And the women found a new grace in that moment to forgive the men in their lives who hurt them.

The women in Mexico are not alone. All over the world, male pride and cultural attitudes of masculine superiority have inflicted horrible wounds on women. For some women, the abuse began early when their fathers or other male relatives sexually molested them. For others, they lost their innocence when uncaring boyfriends raped them. Some women married the man of their dreams, and then woke up after the honeymoon to a nightmare of physical violence that lasted for years. When they dared to speak up about it, even to a Christian pastor, they often were blamed for the abuse or were told to "go home and submit" to more cruelty.

Let me say this to all my sisters in Christ: This abuse is wrong, and I am deeply sorry that the church has failed to address it courageously and forthrightly. God never intended for women to suffer as victims of domestic abuse. This was never God's plan. He created woman in His image, and He intended for man and woman to relate to each other as equals. In marriage, He intended wives to function as co-partners with their husbands—not as some kind of appendage. God never planned for a wife to live under her husband's foot like a domestic servant.

If you have suffered abuse in your past, you have probably been pressured to blame yourself for it. Many women who were sexually abused as children grow up believing that they actually did something sinful that triggered the act of abuse itself. And many women who have endured beatings or other forms of physical cruelty have also been told that the abuse would never have happened if they had been "more submissive" or less critical. These are all lies! God certainly does not blame you for the actions of others. You must break free from the bondage of this deception. The abuse was not your fault.

Perhaps a man never physically or verbally abused you, but you are struggling with feelings of unforgiveness toward a man in your past because of his prejudice, hateful attitudes, chauvinism, insensitivity or pride. God does not want that man's sinful actions to control your life any longer. There is a way to break free from this pain.

The solution is simple: *You must forgive.* There is no option about this. No matter what was done to you, and no matter how many times your husband or another man abused you, you must forgive him from your heart.

This does not mean you must tolerate the behavior (you shouldn't), or that you should stay in an abusive relationship (on the contrary, you should get out of it immediately). Forgiving a man who abused you sexually does not mean he should not be turned in to the police. Forgiving a man who beat you regularly does not mean you should hide his actions.

But forgiveness will be a key to your own emotional freedom. No matter what your father said to you, you must forgive. No matter how that uncaring boyfriend violated you when you were a teenager, you must forgive. No matter how that boss treated you on the job, you must forgive. No matter how that pastor devalued your spiritual gifts because of your gender and went out of his way to deny ministry opportunities to you, you must forgive.

Why is forgiveness so important? Author John Bevere, in his book *The Bait of Satan*, reminds us that the Greek word for "offense," which is *skandalon*, refers to the part of a trap where the bait is attached.[2] This shows us that hurts and offenses become a spiritual trap that the devil uses to ensnare us. Satan knows that if he can lure us to become angry or bitter toward someone, he can hold us in a prison of unforgiveness. And that is where the devil wants us, because hatefulness is the very nature of the devil.

God does not want you to be ensnared in this way. His Word to us, no matter how unjustly we have been treated, is always: "If you have anything against anyone, forgive." (See Matthew 5:24.) If we hold on to our hurts, we choose to live inside a prison of emotional torment. But forgiveness opens the prison door and sets us free.

But how do we know that we have truly forgiven a person? Some people mistakenly assume that they must completely forget the hurtful incident, or they may even try to pretend that it never actually happened. True forgiveness is not about pretending or playing mind games. It is simply a choice we make, by the grace of God, to unconditionally let go of the bitterness we feel in our hearts toward someone who has wronged us.

In his excellent book *Total Forgiveness*, author R. T. Kendall lists several ways to tell whether a person has truly forgiven someone from the heart. According to Kendall's observations, you might want to ask yourself these questions:

- Have you stopped keeping a mental list of the wrongs this person has committed against you?

- Do you still want to "get even" with this person? Do you fantasize about seeing this person punished so he or she "gets what he (she) deserves"? Or do you desire only to see this person obtain mercy for what he (she) did?

- Do you still tell others about the sins of this person so that you can constantly hurt his or her reputation? Or are you now able to speak of this person in a gracious manner?[3]

If you struggle to forgive a man who has hurt you in the past (or who is currently hurting you in some way), then remember the cruelty and abuse that Jesus faced when He was on earth. He was the Son of God, and He deserved to be treated like the King of kings. Yet He was misunderstood and criticized by His own family members, castigated by the religious leaders of His day and mocked by the crowds. The Pharisees scoffed at Him and told Him He had a demon. The barbaric Roman guards spat on Him, tore His flesh off with whips and then executed Him like a common criminal. And the people Jesus came to save stood by His cross and cheered as He was crucified.

What did Jesus say in the face of all this injustice and mistreatment? "Father, forgive them; for they do not know what they are doing" (Luke 23:34). R. T. Kendall says of Jesus' response:

> Asking the Father to forgive them showed that not only had He forgiven them and released them from their guilt, but also that He asked His Father not to punish or take revenge on them. It was not a perfunctory prayer; Jesus meant it. And it was gloriously answered! These offenders were among the very ones Peter addressed on the Day of Pentecost and were converted. (See Acts 2:14–41.)[4]

I would plead with you today: Don't let anger, resentment and bitterness ruin your life. No matter how unjustly you have been treated, you do not have the right to hold any person in judgment.

I meet many women who have been offended by chauvinistic pastors because these men did not provide them a platform for ministry. These men had wrong attitudes. I will not justify their bad behavior. But if you develop a bitter spirit, God will oppose you as you seek other ministry opportunities. Your unforgiveness will prevent you from ever finding complete fulfillment in ministry because people will detect that you are grinding an invisible axe. Unforgiveness is toxic. The anger that seethes inside you will poison your emotions, twist your personality, harm your body and infect people around you.

Let go of your hurts now, and let the Holy Spirit give you a merciful, forbearing heart that is resistant to offense. I invite you to pray this prayer now:

> *Father, You know how _____ hurt me.* (It is important for you to say the name or names aloud.) *You know that what he did to me was not right. But I acknowledge to You now that I do not have a right to hold a grudge against him any longer. I choose today to forgive him. I relinquish all desires to see him punished. I ask instead, Father, that You extend Your mercy to him. Don't give him what he deserves, but reach out to him and forgive his sins—just as You have forgiven mine. In Jesus' name, amen.*

Question #2
Who's the Boss?

My Christian husband often cites biblical passages about being the spiritual head of our house. Does the Bible really say that a husband is the ultimate "boss" in the family? If so, I don't see how my marriage can survive.

It is indeed tragic when a Christian man and woman cannot learn to live in harmony as marriage partners. Both of them have the indwelling Holy Spirit along with access to His infinite reservoir of peace and love. Yet husbands and wives who claim to love God and believe the Bible are divorcing today at an alarming rate. Why?

Obviously we all bring our sinful natures with us into a marriage. Just because two people are Christians does not mean they don't bring all kinds of emotional baggage, sinful habits, addictions, unbiblical mind-sets and generational tendencies into the relationship.

But I believe that another major reason for marital dysfunction in Christian homes is that we have misused and misinterpreted passages in the Bible that refer to a husband's authority. We've encouraged a hierarchy in marriage when God intended *intimacy* and *partnership*. This warped view has created a fragile foundation in many Christian homes, leading to strife, mistrust and, in some cases, abuse.

Let me give an example of how the Bible has been twisted to bring tremendous oppression and emotional pain into women's lives. One woman (I'll call her Cindy) desperately wanted a baby, but she was diagnosed as infertile. Despite many medical procedures and numerous experiments with fertility drugs, nothing changed. Cindy's husband, whom I will call Mark, suggested that the couple consider adoption. But Cindy was not emotionally ready to give up on having her own biological child.

At this point, a caring husband would have tried to understand his wife's disappointment, and he would have responded to her with love and patience. But that is not what happened. Mark decided that since he was "the head of the home," it was his prerogative to make an executive decision. After all, he was the boss. He ruled the roost. He told Cindy that he had decided they should adopt a child—and he demanded that she agree to that arrangement. When she protested, Mark went to the elders of his conservative evangelical church and told them that Cindy was being unsubmissive and rebellious.

Amazingly, the church leaders sided with Mark. They told Cindy, "The Bible makes it clear that you must go along with your husband's decision. He is the leader of your home." When she protested again, the pastors asked her to appear before a group of church members so she could be publicly reprimanded for her insubordination.

Thankfully this is not a typical example. Most church leaders would not have disciplined a woman simply because she wasn't emotionally ready to adopt a child. But such strict, hard-line attitudes about male authority in the home are more common in churches than we would like to admit.

Most conservative, evangelical churches today teach what has come to be known as the doctrine of *male headship*. Although most pastors—and most Christian husbands—don't have a solid grasp of what male headship really means (since such a concept is not clearly defined in the Bible), they defend this truth as if it were a primary tenet of Christian faith. To them, the Bible says that God called husbands to "be in charge" when it comes to family matters. They usually cite Ephesians 5:23: "For the husband is the head of the wife, as Christ also is the head of the church, He Himself being the Savior of the body."

I've asked men I know to tell me what they think male headship means to them. I get a wide variety of vague responses. They include:

- Being the head of my home means I have a responsibility to lead my wife and children in spiritual things like prayer, devotions and Bible study.

- Being the head of my home means I have a priestly responsibility to pray for my wife and children—because God holds me responsible for their spiritual well-being.

- Being the head of my home means the buck stops with me. I'm the boss, and I make the rules.

- Being the head of my home means that when my wife and I can't agree on an issue, I "break the tie."

Some of these responses have a biblical basis. Yes, a husband does indeed have a responsibility to pray for his wife and family. But, on the flip side, doesn't his wife share in that responsibility as her husband's spiritual partner and as a parent? Yes, the husband can and should provide leadership at home. But does this negate his wife's leadership or devalue her counsel?

And what about the "I'm the boss" argument? Is the husband really the "boss" in a marriage?

That is certainly not the way my marriage works. I view my wife, Deborah, as an equal partner. We are one. We share everything. We enjoy a physical, emotional and spiritual unity that is not paralleled in any other human relationship. When we have disagreements, I don't slam my fist on the table and shout, "I am the head of this home, and you must do as I say!" (That would be a dictatorship, not a marriage.) If we cannot reach an agreement, we determine to pray together until we come to a consensus. We defer to one another, and we prefer one another.

There is no passage of Scripture that gives a husband autocratic control in his marriage or that enthrones him in some kind of elevated position of superiority. In fact, Jesus declared that in the kingdom of God, dictatorial control has been replaced by a whole new concept of "servant leadership" marked by humility. (See Matthew 20:25–28.) This means that if a Christian man is bossing his wife around in a rigid, authoritarian manner, he has adopted a pagan leadership style!

God's design for marriage is not a hierarchy, but a loving, nurturing, equal partnership that is characterized by physical intimacy, spiritual oneness and mutual submission. We find this concept taught in Ephesians 5:22–33, where the apostle Paul outlines God's holy purpose for marriage and family. Although this passage is often used to stress the importance of male leadership at home, we've overlooked the main points of the passage, as well as its cultural context and how it was to be applied to a first-century church in Asia Minor.

Biblical Submission in Marriage
Requires *Mutual Submission*

When people talk about submission in marriage, they almost always refer to Ephesians 5:22: "Wives, be subject to your own husbands, as to the Lord." Traditionalists almost always define *submission* as a responsibility of the wife only. But let's not forget what precedes this statement in verse 21: "...and be subject *to one another* in the fear of Christ" (emphasis added).

Did you know that verse 21 sets the tone for the next verse, and that it actually defines the verb used? The verb in verse 22 is not actually there—it is understood according to its context, and for this reason many Bible translations italicize the verb in verse 22. It should be translated like this: *"Submit to one another in the fear of Christ, wives to husbands..."*

In other words, submission should be done *in the spirit of mutual submission.* It is not a one-way street. Paul stressed this mutuality in another passage when he addressed the subject of sexuality in marriage. In 1 Corinthians 7:4 he said, "The wife does not have authority over her own body, but the husband does; and likewise also the husband does not have authority over his own body, but the wife does."

You don't hear too many people quoting that verse in Christian marriage seminars today. Why? Because we have stressed the man's authority so much that we haven't left any room for mutual submission. Yet the Bible says that husband and wife have equal authority in Christ, and they are called to submit to one another whether it is in the intimacy of the bedroom, in difficult parenting decisions or in everyday disagreements.

Headship Does Not Mean "Boss"

We make a serious error in Bible interpretation when we assume that the word *head* in Ephesians 5:23 means "boss" or "ruler." This is not what Paul was teaching when he said, "Wives, be subject to your own husbands, as to the Lord. *For the husband is the head of the wife,* as Christ also is the head of the church, He Himself being the Savior of the body" (vv. 23–24, emphasis added).

Many Bible scholars have pointed out that if Paul had meant this word *head* to mean "leader" or "boss," he would have used the Greek word *archon*. In many passages when "leader" is the intended meaning, *archon* is used. However, in this passage Paul used a more obscure Greek word, *kephale,* which can be translated "source"—as in the "source" or "head" of a river.

Why would Paul say that the husband is the "source" of the wife? Obviously he was making a reference to the Creation story in Genesis, in which Eve was taken out of Adam. The genesis of woman was truly a unique miracle, for she was made of the same essence of the man, taken from his side, yet fashioned into a complementary companion with her own personality and God-given dignity. And because she came from him, they would enjoy a unique bond that no other human or animal could experience. They were separate, yet they were in a mystical union.

Notice that Paul also mentioned the Creation story in Ephesians 5:31 when he quoted a passage from Genesis 2:24: "For this cause a man shall leave his father and mother, and shall cleave to his wife; and the two shall become one flesh." Why did Paul mention a man leaving his parents in this discussion of marriage and submission?

We haven't fully understood this passage because we are ignorant of what it was like to live in the first-century culture of Ephesus. Scholars tell us that in this time period, unmarried women were under the protection and rule of their patriarchal fathers. When a young man wanted to take a woman in marriage, he had to seek permission from her father—and pay a dowry of some kind to win her. Marrying a girl in those days was more like buying property!

Yet even after the two were married, the girl's father often wanted to exercise his control over them. He wanted to be the "boss"of this new marriage. Imagine how difficult it would be to have your father-in-law involved in every decision! In Roman times, this kind of marriage was called "marriage without hand." In some places, the law actually stated that if a married woman spent three nights in her father's home over the course of a year, the father could claim ownership of all of the young couple's possessions![1]

What Paul was really doing in this passage was defining the Christian family. Ancient Middle Eastern culture said that the patriarchal father was the "boss" of the family—including the daughter and her husband. But Paul disagreed; he said that when a man and woman marry, the authority of their parents is nullified. A man and woman begin their new life together as a new unit, enjoying a God-given oneness. The husband is his wife's "head" because woman came from man, and therefore the two enjoy a God-ordained oneness.

Husbands and Wives Are Equals

We also forget that when Paul wrote this letter to the Ephesians, women were basically owned by their husbands. They had no civil rights and were typically dragged around like domesticated animals. They were rarely given any educational opportunities and were viewed simply as servants, sex objects and child-bearers. (And let's not forget that many men in this time period had multiple wives. Polygamy is practiced in any culture or religious system that views women as inferior beings.)

Paul, however, contradicted this pagan view of women and announced that the gospel had brought them a new dignity. He told the men in Ephesus: "So husbands ought also to love their own wives as their own bodies" (Eph. 5:28). He also said to them: "Husbands, love your wives, just as Christ also loved the church and gave Himself up for her" (v. 25).

This was a radical message in Paul's day! Greeks in this time period believed that women were created from animal matter, while they believed men were created from divine matter. To say "Husbands, love your wives" was revolutionary in a culture that did not view women as deserving of love or dignity.

The apostle Peter carried this message further in his first epistle, when he warned men that God would not hear their prayers if they were mistreating their wives. Peter wrote:

> You husbands likewise, live with your wives in an understanding way, as with a weaker vessel, since she is a woman; and grant her honor as a fellow heir of the grace of life, so that your prayers may not be hindered.
>
> —1 PETER 3:7

Notice that Peter does not negate the fact that there are differences between men and women. God wants men to be masculine and women to be feminine. Gender differences are part of the creation order. But man's characteristics—including his physical strength—are not to be used to dominate his wife. On the contrary, God says He will oppose a man if he mistreats his wife or throws his weight around in a chauvinistic way.

In the kingdom of God, the strong must learn to be meek. According to this passage, men who honor their wives as equal partners, esteeming them as "fellow heirs" of God's grace, will enjoy true spiritual power and authority. Meanwhile, those who abuse their fleshly power by trying to be "the boss" will actually lose spiritual authority.

This should be liberating truth for any woman who is currently living with an overbearing husband who thinks he has an innate right to boss her around. If you are in this predicament, your marriage will be healed when both husband and wife come to embrace a truly Christlike understanding of mutual submission, equal partnership and loving oneness.

Question **#3**
Men Behaving Badly

My husband claims he is a Christian, but he has hit me several times, and he is verbally abusive, too. To be honest with you, I am afraid of him. When I have asked a few Christian friends about his behavior, they tell me I should pray for him and learn to submit. What can I do?

First of all, you need to refute the bad counsel you have received from your Christian "friends." I am sure they care about you, but they are sincerely misguided. There is absolutely no place in the Bible that justifies abusive behavior. Neither is there any Scripture in the Bible that calls a woman to submit to physical or emotional abuse from her husband.

Many conservative Christians today—and even some conservative pastors—wrongly have taught that the apostle Paul's words in Ephesians 5:22—"Wives, submit to your husbands..." (NIV)—require wives to tolerate cruel behavior. Many women also have been wrongly taught that the Bible says men are superior (and thus should be obeyed) or that men have better spiritual judgment or are less prone to deception. This, however, is not the spirit of any biblical text.

I have heard horror stories about abused women who sought

18

counseling and were told by pastors to "go home and submit"—even when the husbands were throwing objects at their wives, raping them or sending them to the hospital with broken bones. What irresponsible advice! If any church leader has ever given you counsel like that, he should be confronted and called into account for putting you in danger and for suggesting that God would expect you to tolerate abuse.

It is important that we look closely at what the Bible really means when it entreats women to submit to their husbands. Does this passage about submission in Ephesians 5:22–23 mean that women must do whatever their husbands tell them—even if it is an unreasonable demand? Does it mean that godly husbands are supposed to give their wives orders each day—and that men should expect to be obeyed? Does it mean that women are in a subordinate state compared to their spouses?

Many Christians (including many women) would answer *yes* to all of those questions, but this is not what the Bible requires. In fact, those who promote this notion of male domination or male superiority have embraced a diabolical lie that was hatched in hell and then coated with a religious veneer to make it sound acceptable. Countless women in the church have been wounded as a result.

Paul's words about wifely submission in Ephesians 5:22–31 must be read in context and with the help of the Holy Spirit's revelation. We cannot read our prejudices or preconceived ideas into the passage. Nor can we read our twenty-first-century cultural ideas into it. We must take into consideration the culture Paul was addressing in ancient Ephesus. Let's look at the complete passage carefully:

> Wives, be subject to your own husbands, as to the Lord. For the husband is the head of the wife, as Christ also is the head of the church, He Himself being the Savior of the body. But as the church is subject to Christ, so also

the wives ought to be to their husbands in everything. Husbands, love your wives, just as Christ also loved the church and gave Himself up for her; that He might sanctify her, having cleansed her by the washing of water with the word, that He might present to Himself the church in all her glory, having no spot or wrinkle or any such thing; but that she would be holy and blameless.

So husbands ought also to love their own wives as their own bodies. He who loves his own wife loves himself; for no one ever hated his own flesh, but nourishes and cherishes it, just as Christ also does the church, because we are members of His body. *For this cause a man shall leave his father and mother, and shall cleave to his wife; and the two shall become one flesh.* This mystery is great; but I am speaking with reference to Christ and the church. Nevertheless, let each individual among you also love his own wife even as himself; and let the wife see to it that she respect her husband.

—EPHESIANS 5:22–33, EMPHASIS ADDED

First of all, let's deal with the obvious fact that there are more directives given to husbands than to wives in this passage. The husbands are told to:

1. Love their wives as Christ loved the church (in other words, in a selfless and sacrificial way)

2. Love their wives as their own bodies (in a nurturing manner)

3. Love their wives as they love themselves (with equal respect and mutual concern)

When Paul addresses married couples here, he does not speak

to women only or to men only; rather, he speaks both to husbands and wives because they are partners and team players. He calls them to a place of mutuality, equality and tender devotion.

Paul did not write: "Wives, submit to whatever your husband asks you to do, because the man is in charge." He did not write: "Wives, even if your husband yells at you and makes unreasonable demands and threats, you must keep silent and do what he asks." He did not write: "Wives, even if your husband slaps you across the face and breaks your jaw, you will prove your Christian character by submitting to his behavior and by not saying anything to criticize him." Sadly, though, I have met women who viewed this passage of Scripture as if it should be interpreted in these perverted ways.

A husband should treasure his wife as a gift, love her tenderly, take into consideration her weaknesses and offer her protection, provision, concern and affirmation. If a man is hitting his wife, treating her in a demeaning or degrading way or making harsh demands of her in an authoritarian manner, then obviously he is not loving her as Christ loves the church. He has already violated the spirit of Ephesians 5. And a woman does not have to accept such behavior. In fact, she is putting her own life and the lives of her children at risk if she does not leave the relationship. She has a right and a responsibility to leave.

We also need to consider the cultural context of this passage. One of Paul's main concerns here was not the authority of the husband over the wife, but the order of the family and the unique spiritual unity that married people are supposed to enjoy. (See chapter two.) And as Paul discusses the issue of a married woman's relationship with her husband, notice that the passage culminates by a reference to Genesis 2:24, which states that a man and woman must leave their parents in order to form a new family unit. Why is there a reference to the parents of the married couple in a passage about submission? This is key to interpreting the passage.

In the ancient world, which was typically ruled by patriarchs who sometimes had multiple wives, a father considered his daughter to be his property. When that daughter decided to marry, the father sometimes struggled with releasing control of her. This presented quite a challenge for the young woman's new husband after the wedding—which also was arranged by the parents.

In this patriarchal culture, it was common for the parents of the bride—or perhaps even the parents of the groom as well—to think that they exercised authority over the new couple. To make things more complicated, the new couple most likely lived in the home of one of their parents, or on their property, and they probably worked for the family business. So this put an unusual strain on the marriage relationship.

To correct this situation, Paul pointed out in Ephesians 5 that the woman should "submit" to her husband. This word *submit* (*hupotasso* in the Greek) can also be translated "be attached to." It is a term that denotes connection. In other words, Paul was saying this: "The wife is no longer to answer to her father's authority. She is free from his control. She is now attached to her husband. Now that this new couple is married, they must leave their parents' control and begin a new life together." And this provides the foundation for a Christian view of marriage.

Ephesians 5 is not the only place in the Bible that calls husbands to treat their wives with special love and respect. Another important passage is found in 1 Peter 3:7:

> You husbands likewise, live with your wives in an understanding way, as with a weaker vessel, since she is a woman; and grant her honor as a fellow heir of the grace of life, so that your prayers may not be hindered.

Like Paul, the apostle Peter commanded husbands to show respect and nurturing, protective love to their wives. And he indicated that men who do not treat their wives in this manner will be opposed by God—because their prayers will not be answered. This means that God takes it seriously when a husband mistreats his wife, speaks cruelly to her or resorts to physical violence to get his way. Almighty God does not like domestic abuse, and He will resist the pride in any man who thinks he can get away with it.

What If My Husband Is Abusing Me?

So what should you do if you are suffering some form of abuse in your home? I would offer this advice if you have been subjected to physical abuse that has resulted in bruises, broken bones, black eyes, miscarriage or other physical injuries:

1. Face reality, and admit that you are a battered woman.

Counselors who study domestic violence say that most women blame themselves for the fact that they are abused. You must not submit to the spirit of fear, guilt or manipulation any longer. You need to say to yourself, "This abuse is not right, and I do not have to accept it." You deserve to be treated with respect. Don't believe the lie that says your husband (or boyfriend) is justified to act this way, or that God wants to punish you by making you suffer in an abusive marriage. God hates abuse, and He does not require you to endure it.

Christian psychotherapist Carolyn Holderread Heggen points out that women often learn to tolerate abuse because they have embraced certain heretical religious mind-sets. Three of these beliefs are:

- God intends men to dominate, while women are required to submit.

- Women are morally inferior to men and cannot trust their own judgment.
- Women, in particular, are called to "suffer" in life as the servants of men.[1]

If you have embraced such notions, you must consciously break free from their control. You must renounce false doctrines that cause you to accept abuse. God did not intend for your husband to dominate you, neither did He create you as inferior to your husband. And He did not put you in an abusive relationship in order to punish you or to teach you to suffer. Don't believe the lies!

2. Immediately find a support network.
Share your secret with a pastor, a trusted counselor and some strong Christian friends. Tell them exactly what is going on. Ask them to help you find a place where you can relocate without your husband's knowledge. This could be a battered women's shelter or the home of a friend or relative.

3. Move out of the house.
This seems drastic, but it is the only way to ensure your safety and to begin the process of confronting your husband. Professional counselor John Kie Vining, in his book *When Home Is Where the Hurt Is,* advises women who have children to take them too, along with some cash, car keys and other important papers. You may also want to take any evidence of past injuries, such as photographs or medical records. This will come in handy in the event that you must file a police report.[2]

Most women who are abused over a long period of time do not want to leave their husbands. Often this is because they fear their husbands will kill them or inflict serious injury on them or their children if they find them. This is why you must not attempt to confront your husband's problem yourself. You may simply provoke him to further violence. Studies show that battered women are most likely to be killed if they threaten to leave the marriage. You must leave the situation, but you must not tell him you are planning to separate from him.

4. Ask some men to confront your husband.

This will be the moment of truth. Your husband does not want to expose his sin, and he will go out of his way to protect himself. But if several men can talk with him (after you have left the home), he is more likely to be open to counsel and correction.

Depending on the seriousness of his problem (some abusive husbands are also addicted to drugs or alcohol or may suffer from manic depression), he may have to enter a counseling program, attend accountability classes at a church, go on medication or even go to jail. If he is violent, you should ask the police to intervene. The only way he will find complete restoration is if he is confronted with the reality of his crimes—something best done by other men. Abusive men do not respect women (including women pastors), and they are least likely to become violent when they are around a group of their peers.

5. Find personal healing.

Whether or not you are reunited with your husband after a separation period, you must reclaim your personal worth and overcome the negative emotions that plagued you during the time you were abused. You must rediscover how much God loves you, because the devil used the abuse to convince you that you are ugly, unimportant, repulsive or worthless. Don't believe those lies any longer. Find a healthy church, and ask people there to pray with you for a complete healing of your emotions and memories. If you have children, make sure they also are finding support and regular counseling.

You will not find this healing alone. Find a strong group of Spirit-filled Christians to support you as you walk through this season of restoration. Ask for prayer often. Seek to forgive your husband, realizing that this process of healing takes time. Praying for his healing and restoration will help guard your heart from bitterness.

It is possible that your husband will repent and find the help he needs, thereby saving your marriage. However, it is also possible that your marriage may end in divorce. You must understand that if your husband was abusing you physically, he was already destroying your marriage covenant. You are not bound to remain with him if he has harmed you in this way, and you cannot allow guilt to force you back into a marriage that was already marred by such cruelty.

Some Christians may push you to stay in an abusive marriage by reminding you of Malachi 2:16: "'For I hate divorce,' says the Lord." But it is important for you to read that passage carefully. In the book *Abuse and Religion,* James and Phyllis Alsdurf point out that the next sentence of the verse says, "And I hate a man's covering himself with violence as well as with his garment" (NIV). A footnote in the New International Version says that the verse can be translated: "I hate a man's covering his wife with violence."[3] Yes, God hates divorce, but He also hates wife abuse!

Is physical abuse grounds for divorce? While some traditionalists may argue that "adultery is the only grounds" to end a marriage, the Bible does not address this subject directly. Knowing God's heart for the defenseless, the weak and the disadvantaged, we can confidently assume that the church should never expect a woman to endure beatings or other forms of violence in order to prevent a divorce. Carolyn Holderread Heggen says we need to care more for the abused person than about divorce statistics:

While the Christian community must continue to

uphold the sacredness of the marriage covenant, the church must struggle to understand the permissive will of God in instances where the marriage covenant has already been broken by violence and abuse. The importance of marital permanence must not be elevated above the sanctity of individual personhood or safety. We dare not overlook nor minimize the destructive evils of battery and abuse because of our high regard for the permanence of marriage.[4]

If you must end your marriage, be assured that God wants to give you a new start. He does not want to punish you for something that was not even your fault. Don't listen to the negative voices of shame and self-loathing that have been playing in your head for so long. Meditate on God's Word, stay in close fellowship with other Christians, schedule regular visits with a Bible-based Christian counselor and remind yourself every day that your heavenly Father loves you. Even if you are trapped in a seemingly hopeless relationship, trust God to free you so that you can reclaim your life.

Question #4
Married...
With Children

I am a stay-at-home mother, and I am content to raise my children and focus on my family. I don't sense any kind of special calling to preach or pastor. Don't you think it is unhealthy to push women to leave the home and pursue ministry?

I am certainly not "pushing" women to abandon their marriages or their children in order to have a ministry. The family was God's idea, and those who have been blessed with children have a sobering responsibility to meet their physical needs, nurture them with love and teach them how to know and serve the Lord faithfully. Parenting can be one of the most rewarding experiences in life. If you are currently a full-time mother and feel this is your God-given calling for a season, then you are blessed with a wonderful charge. Your children and husband are fortunate that you are so passionate about the responsibility of motherhood.

But let's also remember that not every woman feels the same calling you do, and you must leave room for her to follow the Holy Spirit, just as those with a different calling shouldn't criticize you for adopting the traditional role of stay-at-home mom. There are all kinds of women in the church today:

- Some are single women who may or may not ever get married and have children. Single people, in fact, are the fastest-growing demographic segment in evangelical churches today.

- Many women are divorced, widowed or are living in single-parent situations because of an out-of-wedlock pregnancy. For them, "staying home" and raising a family in the traditional sense is not an option because of financial realities.

- Some women who have children feel a calling from God to be in the workplace, and they and their husbands have worked out arrangements for childcare that fit their needs. In the past, churches have done a poor job of ministering to working women, either because we felt they were abandoning their families or perhaps because we were intimidated by their educational or professional achievements.

- Some women with children do, in fact, feel a call to full-time ministry, and we should do everything we can to support them as they seek to discern God's plan for their lives. It is not the norm for a woman with small children to be called into full-time ministry, but why not? God certainly can do whatever He pleases.

In the Bible, God used an enslaved concubine named Esther, a barren wife named Hannah, an elderly widow named Anna, a teenage girl named Mary, an immoral divorcee from Samaria and even a harlot named Rahab to accomplish His will. Why then should we be surprised if God wants to use a woman who still has children at home?

The most important thing for you to remember is that whether you are single or married, working in an office or caring for small children at home, you are called to be a minister of the gospel. We are all ministers "of reconciliation" (2 Cor. 5:18), and we all carry within us the treasure of His Holy Spirit in our earthly jars of clay (2 Cor. 4:7).

Just because you are responsible for children in the home does not mean that is your only duty. Don't fall into the trap of limiting yourself to your *role* as a wife and mother. You cannot say to God, "Now that I am a stay-at-home mom, I'll just fulfill my role as mother for the next eighteen years, and then after that I'll serve You in some other way." If you are seeking the Lord diligently, you will be surprised at the ways He may call you to minister from the seemingly insignificant corner of your domestic world. If you have chosen to "seek first the kingdom of God" (Matt. 6:33, NKJV), then you can expect that He will give you kingdom assignments while you are in this season of life.

This happened to one of the great heroes of the faith, Susanna Wesley, the mother of revivalists John and Charles Wesley. In the austere culture of England in the 1700s, women like Susanna stayed close to home. Her children consumed her life, and she did not have any particular aspirations for a public ministry, at least in the early years of her life. But her spiritual impact on her community was remarkable, and the revivalist passion that burned in her heart eventually helped ignite the First Great Awakening.

Once, while her husband, Samuel, was away during the winter of 1711, she began a Bible study in her home that quickly attracted a group of more than thirty parishioners from her husband's Anglican church. While she remained apologetic about the fact that a woman was leading these meetings (this was highly unusual in her day), her "awakening sermons" were soon attracting crowds of two hundred, and she was forced to turn people away from her home because there was no space left.

Her husband actually questioned Susanna's spiritual activities, probably out of annoyance that his congregation did not respond as enthusiastically to his own preaching. She told Samuel that she sensed a spiritual duty to save souls:

> I doubt if it is proper for me to present the prayers of the people to God. Last Sunday I would fain have dismissed them before prayers; but they begged so earnestly to stay, I durst not deny them.[1]

Susanna had reservations about her ministry activities because of her gender, and she rarely felt supported by her husband. But her son John referred to her later in his life as a "preacher of righteousness," and it was most likely her godly influence that opened him to the idea of using women preachers in his Methodist revival campaigns. As he grew older, Wesley openly encouraged women to enlist in public ministry, and some of his best circuit-riding evangelists were female. One of them, Sarah Crosby, typically preached four times a day beginning at 5 A.M. One year she traveled 960 miles on horseback, held 120 public services and led 600 private meetings.[2]

Though Susanna Wesley never traveled through the English countryside like Sarah Crosby, she might have done so if she had lived in another time period. She once told her husband in a letter: "Though I am not a man, nor a minister, yet if my heart were sincerely devoted to God, and I was inspired with a true zeal for His glory, I might do somewhat more than I do."[3]

Long before it was acceptable for mothers to be in the ministry, Catherine Booth set the standard by breaking all the religious rules of her day. She and her revivalist husband, William, brought their children along with them as they planted churches, established rescue missions and turned England upside down for Christ in the 1880s. All of their children grew up to serve in The Salvation Army as adults. Once, when a mother asked Catherine how she got her children converted so early, the spunky preacher replied:

> I have been beforehand with the devil. I have not allowed my children to become preoccupied with the things of the world before I have got the seed of the Kingdom well in.[4]

One of America's most notable revivalists was not only a mother, but also a mother whose heart had been broken by tragedy. Maria Woodworth-Etter felt a call to ministry early in life, but the Disciples of Christ did not allow women to engage in any form of preaching or ministry work. She married and had six children, but five of them died in childhood. Yet somehow this broken woman was able to overcome her grief, and she eventually became an itinerant evangelist with a wide following. As many as twenty-five thousand people attended some of her holiness meetings held in Indiana, Massachusetts and Illinois in the early 1900s, and people she prayed for testified of miracles and healings. How amazing that God would use a brokenhearted mother to pour out upon America the first Pentecostal revival marked by divine healing.

Maria Woodworth-Etter did not necessarily want to surrender to a call to the ministry. She was afraid of crowds; the thought of standing in front of an audience and preaching horrified her. She also was acutely aware that religious people would view her public ministry as being scandalous because she was a woman. To make matters worse, her husband and adult daughter opposed her when she talked about the possibilities of beginning a traveling ministry.

What convinced Woodworth-Etter to break out of her comfort zone was a supernatural vision of hell:

> I was very timid, and bound as with chains in a man-

fearing spirit. When I arose to testify I trembled like a leaf, and began to make excuses—"O God, send someone else!" Then the Lord in a vision caused me to see the bottomless pit open in all its horror and woe. There was weeping and wailing and gnashing of teeth. It was surrounded by a great multitude of people who seemed unconscious of their danger, and without a moment's warning they would tumble into this awful place…

This vision left quite an impression on my mind. When the Spirit of God was striving with me to talk or pray in the meeting, I would resist as long as I could. Then the awful vision would rise before me, and I would see souls sinking into eternal woe. The voice of Jesus would whisper, "I am with you; do not be afraid." Then I would be on my feet or knees in a moment. I would forget everything but the love of God and dying souls.[5]

You may not be called to preach publicly like Maria Woodworth-Etter, but God does want to share with you His burden for lost souls. He wants to use your mother's heart to touch a broken world. Caring for your own youngsters may be your first priority, but don't close your heart to Him.

God may want to visit you in the night while you are nursing an infant to sleep and call you to pray for a city or a nation. He may want to use you to reach the children in your apartment complex or the other mothers in your neighborhood. He may call you to take your children with you as you minister to the elderly or to a shelter for battered women. He may ask you to volunteer at a crisis pregnancy clinic where you can mentor young girls who have never known a mother's love. He may have a spiritual adventure waiting for you—but you must step outside the security of your domestic world to see His plan.

Let's remember that in the Old Testament, when God's people were called to assemble before Him to hear the prophets' words or to repent corporately for national sin, even the mothers with nursing babes were required to be in attendance (Joel 2:16). You are not excused either. Don't let your role as a mother stop you from sharing your faith or from seeking God for revival. In this critical hour, the church needs every believer to participate in the Holy Spirit's plan to reach the world.

Question #5
Diapers and Day Care

I have small children, and I am getting conflicting advice. Some Christians say I am disobeying God if I work outside the home. Others say it's OK. What should I do?

This is probably one of the most common struggles Christian women face today, yet the church has not always offered compassion or practical solutions. In fact, we are notorious for giving women simplistic, pat answers laced with mean-spirited judgments. Often the issue of working mothers becomes so divisive that it splits churches.

I understand your conflict because my wife, Deborah, and I faced this issue when our first daughter, Margaret, was born in 1985. We asked all the difficult questions: Should we try to live on one income? If my wife went to work, who would watch Margaret? Is institutionalized day care harmful to children? Would we bond properly with our children if they stayed with a babysitter all day? Should we raise our family the traditional way—with my wife staying home full time—or should we become a two-income household?

Every Christian couple needs to ask these questions. Children are a precious gift and a huge responsibility—and you only get one chance to raise them. We realized the day we brought our first baby home from the hospital that our kids would be a priority from that moment on. We knew we couldn't just fit them into a convenient compartment of our lives. Children require a huge investment of time, money and emotional energy, yet our culture today does not applaud the selflessness and sacrifice that successful parenting requires.

My wife and I asked many questions, read lots of books about child rearing, sought counsel from friends and prayed often for God's direction. Ultimately we felt the traditional model would work best for us. Deborah did not want to start a career at that time in her life, and my income was substantial enough for us to survive (although we had to accept that fact that we would never have as nice a house as the two-income couples we knew). Deborah and I both wanted several children, but after the fourth girl arrived we decided that our family unit was complete. Because my wife majored in child development in college, she decided she wanted to be as hands-on as possible with our little ones.

That may sound like a traditional family, but you have to understand that I did not force my wife to stay home because I thought this was "a woman's role." If Deborah had wanted to start a career in those early years, we would have moved in that direction. (Believe me, there were times when I would have appreciated a second income.) But we tried to practice mutual submission in our marriage because we believe that is the biblical model. We learned to defer to each other and to consider each other's preferences. We prayed about important decisions, and when disagreements arose, we hashed things out and reached a consensus.

Also, just because I was the only wage earner in the family did not mean that I didn't help with parenting responsibilities. When our children were small I changed diapers, vacuumed the house, washed dishes and took the girls out for day-long outings so my wife could have her own free time. Those days convinced me that stay-at-home mothers deal with more stress on the job than most executives do.

The traditional model worked for us—but it is not the answer for everyone. Christians make a huge mistake when they insist that the only biblical family model is the stay-at-home mother. Although it is certainly ideal for a child to have continuous parental attention during the first few years of his or her life, this is not always possible for many families—nor is it what all women feel called to do. Single mothers certainly cannot stay home all day, even when their children are toddlers. And many married couples I know cannot pay their monthly bills with one income. These people certainly aren't helped when the church tells them God requires all mothers to stay home.

Parenting Guidelines for Consideration

As you pray for God's direction in your situation, I would suggest that you consider these helpful guidelines:

1. Parenting is not just a mother's responsibility.

Gretchen Gaebelein Hull tells the story of a missionary whose board objected to his wife attending college classes in the evening. When he asked why this would be wrong, the board explained that when the wife was away from home, the man would have to change his infant's diapers—and this was viewed as "role reversal." Says Hull: "The critics failed to see that changing diapers is not a woman's role or a man's role, but an act of simple compassion for a helpless child...For a man to refuse to assume the responsibility when necessary or appropriate is to show callous insensitivity."[1]

There is no verse in the Bible that says women are supposed to shoulder the majority of childcare. It does not say that only mothers change diapers, sing babies to sleep, entertain toddlers or give them baths. To assume that childcare is only "a woman's work" is chauvinistic—and rooted in the pagan idea that women are slaves who do nothing but provide sex and do housework. Furthermore, psychologists are only now realizing the importance of a father's influence in the early years of a child's life. Fathers who refuse to cuddle with their kids, play games with them or get involved in other nurturing activities are actually harming their children emotionally.

I have a good friend named Tessie who is an executive with a Christian publishing company. When her first child was born, she and her husband, David, prayed about whether she should quit her job to stay home with their newborn. But they felt the Lord directed them to do something unique: Tessie would continue working full time (after a lengthy maternity leave), while David—a real estate agent who works out of his home—would shoulder the bulk of the responsibility for caring for his son in his early years.

The arrangement proved to be a blessing for everyone. Tessie was able to bring home her salary (and fulfill what she felt was a ministry calling), David enjoyed much more time with his son than most American fathers do, and their little boy certainly didn't suffer for it. As David's real estate business grew more successful, he and Tessie enrolled their son in a Christian nursery school.

David and Tessie were not breaking a biblical law by choosing this path. They were not "reversing roles." They were simply following the Holy Spirit's direction in their unique situation. Yet many traditional Christians would condemn this arrangement simply because it conflicts with a rigid religious mind-set of what men and women do in the family.

We need to remember that the stay-at-home model of child raising is a relatively new phenomenon. In biblical times, both mothers and fathers worked from the home, and the mother was often in the fields all day while older siblings or relatives watched the children. (Oftentimes even very young children also were working in the fields.) In those days, fathers had much more opportunity to interact with their children than modern dads who drive thirty minutes or more to an office or factory and sometimes only see their children on weekends.

This absentee-father scenario is certainly not healthy for the children involved, but the church today seems to ignore it (and sometimes even applauds it) while at the same time heaping guilt on women who feel called to the workplace.

2. Safe, healthy childcare alternatives are available.

I have a friend, Valerie, who is a single mother. Economic realities made it impossible for her to stay home all day and care for her daughter. (And so far no church has volunteered to pay all her bills and cover her mortgage each month so that she could do this!) Yet Valerie was able to enroll her child in a top-rated Christian school, and the school has regularly awarded a scholarship to help with tuition costs. Today, Valerie's daughter makes the honor roll, she is active in her church youth group, she won a national public speaking contest, and she competed in the national Junior Miss Young Woman of Excellence pageant and won.

Your young children will not be ruined for life if they stay in a day-care center several hours a day. If you must place your child in the care of others, the important thing is to find a wholesome Christian atmosphere where the spiritual as well as physical and emotional needs of your child are a priority. That may be in a home with relatives or a friend or in a professional childcare facility. Check references, and ask for referrals from other parents.

Trust the Lord to direct your decision. Don't let false guilt or the criticism of others stop you from choosing day care if this is the path you must take.

If you are a single parent, you must remember that God will go out of His way to provide for you. Psalm 68:5 says that He will be a Father to the fatherless. He also promises to set "the solitary in families" (Ps. 68:6, NKJV). If you trust Him, He will provide a means for you to find affordable childcare that is not only healthy for your child but also spiritually enriching.

3. Women who choose to stay home with young children can start careers later.

Golda Meir served in political positions for forty-five years before she was elected prime minister of Israel in 1969. Respected by world leaders and affectionately known as "Mother Courage" by her own people, she fought arduously for the Zionist cause and signed Israel's declaration of independence in 1948. Yet this champion of freedom faced the same struggle millions of women have faced ever since they were given the right to own property and earn wages. She had to balance career and family.

Most people don't know that Mrs. Meir, a Ukrainian Jew who got her college education in the United States, chose to stay home with her two children when they were young. While living in kibbutzes in Palestine, she did other people's laundry to help meet her family's expenses. She once said of a mother's conflict: "At work, you think of the children you've left at home. At home, you think of the work you've left unfinished. Such a struggle is unleashed within yourself, your heart is rent."[2]

It's a tough choice. If you are wrestling with whether to work outside the home or not, you and your husband must decide that together. Don't be motivated by guilt, fear or religious judgments. Let the Holy Spirit lead you. But you must know that God might ask you to place your career ambitions on hold while your children are young—and if He requires this, you should embrace God's perfect will and trust that He will honor your sacrifice.

At the same time, however, don't let go of your dreams. Your children will be in college quicker than you think—and it will be time to reevaluate and reprioritize. There are seasons in a woman's life. Countless women who were stay-at-home moms decided later to launch their own businesses or enroll in college or seminary.

I also know many women who entered the ministry after their children left home. One of them, popular charismatic Bible teacher Iverna Tompkins, waited until her son was seventeen before she began accepting speaking engagements that required her to travel. Today, at a time in life when many women are thinking about retirement, Iverna is more active than most women half her age.

Thetus Tenney, mother of best-selling author Tommy Tenney, travels the world today preaching in churches and conferences. She admits that when God required her to stay home when her two children were small, she had to fight resentment. But the conflict was resolved for her when she realized that God had a special plan for her during those years of tending to little ones:

> Before going to bed each night, I would set the house in order for the next day. Then I'd wake up very early the next morning and have several hours of undisturbed prayer and study before my motherly duties demanded my attention. I read many books. I even read Bible commentaries. This was a season which, in retrospect, passed much more quickly than it seemed at the time.
>
> Little did I realize, while taking care of my primary responsibility as a young mother, that I had also been

given an opportunity that would develop my future ministry of teaching and writing. Those years of study became the foundation for my life's work.[3]

If God does call you to put some of your dreams on hold because of your family, it will not be time wasted. Embrace those years as a time for character building and refining. The lessons you learn while serving others in the hiddenness of your home will prepare you for God's next assignment.

Question #6
The Working Woman's Dilemma

Women in my church have criticized me because I am a professional businesswoman. They told me I am out of God's will because I am not allowing my husband to be the true head of my home by providing for our needs. How should I respond to them?

I am sorry you have been misjudged because of your choice to pursue a career. I realize that this criticism came from Christians, but you must recognize that if they condemned you, they were not reflecting the true heart of God. The Bible does not say that all women must stay home and spend their lives in the kitchen. But this what a lot of conservative religious people believe. Don't let their criticism offend you. And don't let it stop you from fulfilling your God-given dreams.

Since the fall of humanity, women have suffered oppression and subjection, and for centuries men expected their wives to live sequestered lives. They were forced to be household slaves whose only jobs in life involved cooking meals, cleaning house, performing backbreaking tasks in the fields and bearing and raising children. This harsh view of women is still the norm in many developing countries where Islam, Buddhism or Hinduism shapes the culture. Under the harsh rule of the Taliban in Afghanistan, before the war on terrorism began in 2001, girls were not even allowed to attend school because the men believed that women should only learn to cook and sew. Women were forced to live indoors, and if they ventured outside without covering their entire bodies with a floor-length veil, they could be beaten or arrested.

Jesus came to set women free from this oppression. He elevated women to a place of dignity and equality with men. That's why women are always lifted to a higher place in society when the gospel is preached. Only in predominantly Christian nations have women gained full civil rights, along with the right to vote, own property, hold political office, own businesses and pursue higher education.

We see this elevated view of women illustrated in Proverbs 31:10–11, a classic passage that eloquently portrays the "virtuous wife." This woman was far ahead of her time. She was by no means the "traditional woman" of her day.

During the Old Testament period when Proverbs 31 was written, most women were uneducated. They spent the majority of their time gathering water, cooking meals and performing strenuous agricultural tasks while they labored to raise several children at the same time. Some also had to share their homes with the other wives of their one husband!

Yet the woman described in this Bible passage is actually what we would call a "working woman." She is involved in a home business involving textile manufacturing (v. 13). She employs other women to help her (v. 15), and she sells her wares on the open market (v. 24). She is also involved in buying and selling real estate and in agricultural development (v. 16). And in her spare time she devotes herself to charitable projects, most likely funding them through her own profitable ventures (v. 20).

This woman is praised not only for her kindness and her godly character. She is honored because of her entrepreneurial skills, her diligence at work, her resourcefulness and her business acumen. And notice these verses in the passage:

> The heart of her husband trusts in her, and he will have no lack of gain. She does him good and not evil all the days of her life...She considers a field and buys it; from her earnings she plants a vineyard...She senses that her gain is good.
>
> —PROVERBS 31:11–12, 16, 18

Notice that Proverbs 31 does not focus on this woman's cooking or her child-raising skills, although it is implied that she is involved in these activities. The passage almost exclusively focuses on her business involvement. She is a merchant, and a successful one at that. So much so that she becomes wealthy, and her contribution to the family income brings notoriety and respect to her husband—which he passes along to her by saying, "Give her the reward she has earned" (v. 31, NIV).

So here, buried in this Old Testament passage, is God's heart for women. It was never His plan for His daughters to be locked in the kitchen or the nursery. Although some women prefer not to pursue careers when their children are small—and this is certainly a laudable decision when it is economically feasible—it is not a biblical mandate for all women.

Conservative Christians today often imply that women should make home and motherhood their first or only priority. Sometimes motherhood is even praised as "a woman's highest calling." It sounds so family-friendly, but such a mind-set is insensitive, especially to women who are either unmarried or childless, and it can be hurtful to women who are infertile. If motherhood is God's highest calling, does that mean unmarried women will never attain to God's plan for their lives? And for that matter, who said that a woman with children should not pursue other interests or goals that fall outside of her maternal duties?

Of course motherhood is a special calling. And full-time mothers deserve our applause. But where did we get the idea that motherhood has been set apart as God's "highest" place for women? This is certainly not a biblical view, since many women in the Bible who are lauded for their faith did not have children.

In the early 1900s, many Christian leaders rejected the women's suffrage movement and vigorously opposed the idea of women becoming involved in the political process. Some traditionalists feared that if women began voting, the family would be destroyed. Others felt the nation would become "feminized" by the sudden influx of women in public life. So, in order to protect their traditional world, religious people began to emphasize the importance of home and motherhood. Even the Victorian-style art of the day—showing tender scenes of mothers and children reading, playing and embracing—bolstered the odd notion that society could be preserved if women would stay out of public life. These beautiful images were actually a form of cultural propaganda.

This image continued into the 1950s, when the so-called "June Cleaver" model became the norm for American housewives. The church continued to promote the idealistic notion that women are better off staying home, ironing clothes, baking cookies and attending garden parties while their husbands go to the office.

None of this was based on a biblical model. It was, in fact, a holdover from the days of Victorian England. During that time period, when men began to work in industrial jobs that took them outside the home and away from the family farm for the first time, women who had wealth were urged to stay indoors. The idea was that women, with their delicate nature, could somehow preserve the morals of society if they lived in a cloistered world of tea parties, tight corsets and taffeta gowns. The women of Victorian England would have made a more powerful impact on their society if they had been a part of it, rather than hiding in their parlors.

If people in your church are imposing this narrow mind-set on you, suggesting that it is wrong for a Christian woman to enter the business world, then stand your ground and maintain your liberty in Christ.

Serving the Lord as a Working Woman

Here are some other helpful steps that will enable you to serve the Lord in your profession:

1. Discover your calling as Christ's witness in the marketplace.

The task of evangelizing your nation is not going to be accomplished by full-time preachers alone. In fact, most people discover faith as a result of a one-on-one encounter with a friend, often at their job. God wants to use you in your place of business to influence others for Him.

In the United States in the early years of the twenty-first century, the fastest-growing segment of the economy was fueled by new businesses started by women entrepreneurs. Imagine what could happen if many of these female business owners were Bible-believing Christians who understood the need for integrity, honesty and faithfulness in all business transactions. How would this transform what we know of as the "good ol' boys' club" in corporate America—a club that has been known for back room deals, bribery, extortion and Enron-style scandals? Could it be that God could use female corporate executives to lead the United States back to righteousness?

Many church leaders today believe that the greatest evangelism opportunities in this new century will occur in the marketplace, led not by full-time ministers but by what they call "marketplace ministers"—Christian businesspeople who carry their faith into the working world. Many of these business owners will be females.

2. Use your resources for Christ's kingdom.

The Proverbs 31 woman would never have been able to "[open] her arms to the poor" or "[extend] her hands to the needy" (v. 20, NIV) if she had not first made profits from her business. God blessed her and made her a blessing. If God has called you into the business world, it is possible that He wants to channel wealth through you that will build His kingdom. Be open to creative ideas that will enable you to achieve financial success for the cause of Christ.

We need women today who are free to think big. Don't allow the restrictions of the past to box you in. God's businesswomen must be free to do exploits for Him. As a working woman, you may be called to channel money into kingdom projects that feed the poor, eradicate disease, build hospitals and orphanages, fund missionaries and Christian publishing projects and transform nations. Your business, in fact, might actually be used in a developing nation to bring jobs and economic prosperity—and perhaps lift other women out of poverty. Don't limit God in how He could use your entrepreneurial skills.

And don't limit God's creativity in you. God has used women inventors in the past to bless the world. Women invented windshield wipers, modern eyeglasses, emergency flares, the bobbinless sewing machine, the paper bag, several cancer drugs, including AZT (the drug that slows the progress of the AIDS virus), and a feeding apparatus for disabled people.[1] What further advances will be made in medicine, technology and science when more women feel released to be inventive?

3. Seek to influence society as a reformer.

In Nigeria, a nation I have visited twice in recent years, women still suffer from harsh cultural oppression. Although they won the right to vote in the 1960s, they still lack many basic human rights, including the right to protection from domestic abuse (which is quite common, even in Christian homes). Only recently have women emerged on the political scene, but that is beginning to change.

One bright spot on Nigeria's horizon is Dora Akunyili, a Christian woman who was appointed in 2001 to head Nigeria's National Agency for Food and Drug Administration and Control. Immediately she went on a crusade to stop the problem of fraud in the pharmaceutical industry. Before her reform campaign began, drug companies were manufacturing useless medicines and selling them in order to make an illegal profit. The problem had become so prevalent that Nigeria developed an international reputation for being deceptive in its business dealings. But Mrs. Akunyili decided to put a stop to it, and she has led numerous raids on labs that were producing fake drugs.

Her campaign has been waged at a great personal cost, but she has remained fearless. She must travel with bodyguards because her life has been threatened so often by the corrupt pharmaceutical bosses. Yet she told a Nigerian Christian magazine in 2002 that she feels God is protecting her and empowering her to bring morality and the rule of law back to Nigerian society. She said, "To me, a criminal can never be big. A criminal has no power."[2]

Similar voices of reform have emerged in nearby Uganda. After a revival of Christianity began to sweep through that African country in the 1990s, many brave women of faith have been elected to political office there. One of them, Miria Mtembe, has been appointed to oversee a new department that is focused on improving morality in the nation. As director of the Ministry of Ethics and Integrity, she is calling for sexual purity, marital faithfulness and an end to corruption in a nation that has been devastated by the AIDS epidemic. [3]

My question is this: Where are the female reformers today? Why do we not see more women crying out for justice, righteousness and societal transformation? Does God want you to step into this role?

We have already looked at the Proverbs 31 woman and discussed her ability to bless the poor because of her wealth and her business savvy. But we also need to pay attention to another woman in Proverbs—the brave herald of Proverbs 8. This woman, who is a personification of God's wisdom, is portrayed as a bold reformer who cries out from the central city square. She is stationed at "the gates leading to the city"—which denotes the seat of government in Bible times. Her message is one of repentance:

> To you, O men, I call out;
> I raise my voice to all mankind.
> You who are simple, gain prudence;
> You who are foolish, gain understanding.
> Listen, for I have worthy things to say;
> I open my lips to speak what is right.
> —Proverbs 8:4–6, NIV

Where are the Proverbs 8 women of our day? We need more voices like hers in the city square. We need Christian women in every field—medicine, education, government, law, science, business and the arts—who will call out to society, blow the whistle on corruption and bring the principles of honesty, justice, mercy and integrity to bear on all institutions.

We saw a great number of female Christian reformers arise in previous generations. The abolitionist movement, which brought an end to slavery in the United States, was led for the most part by

Spirit-empowered women who knew that the Bible did not justify oppression. A few years later, women like Frances Willard of the Women's Christian Temperance Union led a national revolt against the vices associated with alcohol.

Yet today, many Christian women seem out of touch with the problems of society. They have been sequestered inside their homes, focused only on their own families, seemingly powerless to offer a relevant message to our troubled culture. I believe that is partly because we have encouraged women to be silent when we need them on the front lines.

I challenge you to break the mold. I hope you will seek God for the courage to transform your community, city and nation, and that He will empower you to be a voice for righteousness.

Question #7
Dragging Your Husband Along

My husband attends church, but he has no prayer life and struggles in his relationship with God. I feel guilty because I am more spiritual than he is. After all, isn't he supposed to function as the "priest" of my home?

First of all, let's deal directly with the idea that your husband is "priest of the home." When anyone ever mentions that phrase in conversation with me, I immediately ask: "Can you show me that verse in the Bible?"

Guess what? It's not in there!

There is no Scripture verse that says, "The husband is priest of the home." Nothing even close! Yet there are countless women who believe it is a biblical concept, and the phrase is repeated continually in American pulpits as if it were Scripture. It is, in fact, a very unbiblical viewpoint—because God's Word never indicates that a husband is supposed to hear God for his wife (as if she cannot hear God for herself) or represent his wife to God (as if she cannot approach His presence herself). To suggest that a woman needs her husband to be her priest or mediator would be to imply that the blood of our only true Mediator, Jesus Christ, is not enough to grant a woman the free gift of righteousness.

For that reason, anyone who teaches that a wife must go to God "through" her husband's priestly ministry is teaching heresy. The Bible says that all believers, whether single or married, are priests unto God (1 Pet. 2:9). A woman whose husband is not a Christian still has her own relationship with God. She is, in fact, the priest of her home! The same applies to you—even though your husband is not as spiritual as you wish he were at this time. You can enjoy your own relationship with God regardless of where your husband is spiritually—and you have access to all of the Lord's covenant benefits.

You say your husband is not as spiritual as you are? Welcome to the real world. There are many women today in your situation. Don't fall into the trap of thinking that your life must measure up to some kind of artificial standard before you can truly be an effective Christian. God can work through you now—even if your husband is a backslider or an unbeliever.

Some Christian women have impossibly idealistic expectations about marriage and family. They were told by a friend, a parent, a pastor or a church leader that in the "perfect" Christian home, the man is the spiritual leader. He goes up on the mountain of God, like Moses, and hears the word of the Lord. Then he comes down from the glory of that encounter, with his face shining, and tells his wife and children how they should live.

The wife, of course, kneels at her husband's feet each night and washes them while he instructs her. The children sit quietly by the fireplace in their matching pajamas and listen to their father's wisdom. When he is finished with his devotional message, they say their prayers, recite their memorized Bible verses and then quietly march in single file to their bedrooms for the night.

Excuse me? I don't have to tell you that such a scene is not

53

normal. When most Christian fathers return home from work each night, they have not been basking in a cloud of God's glory. Whether the wife was home preparing dinner or just arriving home from her own job, she is most likely not in the mood to sit at her husband's feet and listen to a lecture. And whoever said little children can sit through a thirty-minute sermon without fidgeting never had any kids of their own!

That scenario is not realistic. Real marriages don't work that way, and we should not uphold this ideal as a standard. Husbands often come home from work tired; wives are often frazzled from their own day at the office or from the frenzy of childcare; and children get into trouble, break things, track mud through the house and sometimes have to be spanked because of bad attitudes. Real life happens, and it gets even more challenging when the youngsters hit their teen years.

Many Christian women are married to husbands who are not as spiritual as they are. This is how life is. I wish I could promise you that if you follow four easy steps, your husband will become a spiritual giant overnight, or he will start praying with you every night, or he will even begin prophesying during church services. But that may not happen! And it does not have to happen in order for you to experience God for yourself. Your husband's lack of spirituality cannot prevent you from achieving spiritual maturity.

I hope you don't think I am making light of your situation. I know it can be very frustrating—and painful as well—to feel disconnected spiritually with your spouse. But you cannot allow your own passion for God to make you feel guilty. And you certainly cannot blame yourself for your husband's lukewarm faith.

Many Christians have unrealistic standards and expectations about how life is supposed to be. They assume that a victorious Christian life means freedom from struggles, scandals, pain and suffering. There is no room in their world for sickness, miscarriage, crib death, divorce, teenage rebellion, out-of-wedlock pregnancy, rape, lawsuits, bankruptcy, car accidents, delinquent children, learning disabilities, cancer, racism, secret addictions, eating disorders or the premature death of a friend or relative.

Yet I know many, many Christians who have to deal with these and other traumatic problems at some point in their lives. Those who are crushed by their circumstances are always the ones who did not look at their problems realistically. They never read the Book of Job. They never embraced the fact that our spiritual journey would include trials, affliction and hardship.

Those who overcome and experience true victory, on the other hand, are the ones who trusted God to give them special grace to handle whatever circumstances they faced.

Helping Your Husband Grow Spiritually

I would encourage you to consider taking these four steps as you face life with a husband who does not know the Lord or who lacks spiritual passion.

1. Thank God for your husband.

He may not be a spiritual firebrand, but you can surely think of several positive qualities you see in him. Perhaps he is a good listener. Maybe he is an excellent handyman. When is the last time you thought about his unique skills, abilities and character traits? Or have you been fretting constantly about the fact that he doesn't measure up to your expectations?

Learn to focus your attention on his strengths so that you do not develop a bitter attitude toward him. If you allow yourself to become critical, you will actually hinder him from growing in his relationship with the Lord and put your marriage at risk, too.

The Bible often speaks about the power of a wife's words. You can be constructive or destructive, depending on whether you allow the Holy Spirit to temper your conversation and attitudes. Proverbs 14:1 says, "The wise woman builds her house, but the foolish tears it down with her own hands."

Solomon wrote, "The contentions of a wife are a constant dripping" (Prov. 19:13). He also said that it was better for a husband to live "in a corner of a roof" or "in a desert land" than in a house shared "with a contentious and vexing woman" (Prov. 21:9, 19). He did not say this because he was a woman-hater. No husband enjoys being scrutinized and criticized by his wife if she offers constant complaining. A man's reaction to this negativity will always be to withdraw, to become passive or to seek intimacy and solace outside of the home. A wife can actually drive her husband away if she insists on constant faultfinding.

Learn to thank the Lord for your husband, and then offer regular compliments and encouragement. And if you can't think of anything positive to say, learn to bite your lip and say nothing. There is a time and place for correction, but that time does not roll around as frequently as we think.

2. Ask God for a prayer strategy, and then pray for your husband consistently.

The Holy Spirit holds the answer to your husband's problems and challenges. Rather than striving in your own flesh to change his attitudes or to fuel his spiritual passion, let God do it. All you need to do is ask Him. Then simply believe that He is at work.

Your husband may struggle spiritually because of some traumatic experience he has never told you about. He may have disqualified himself from ever being what he considers "a good Christian" because of something he did twenty years ago. Guilt and condemnation always cause a person to withdraw from God.

I have counseled with many men who face serious emotional

and psychological problems. Because of the pressures from society (and the church) to appear strong, men tend to bury their hurts because to talk about them openly would be to admit failure. If they have been sexually abused or struggle with embarrassing sins like masturbation, pornography, adultery, homosexual desires or compulsive addictions such as gambling or alcoholism, they may simply bury their pain and lose touch with their emotions.

This invariably will take its toll on a man's spiritual life. The guilt and shame associated with his unresolved problems will prevent him from enjoying a healthy relationship with God. When you pray for your husband, ask God to break through any shame or guilt that has created a wall of separation.

3. Encourage your husband to be in fellowship with other Christian men.

I hope you are not threatened by the fact that men don't necessarily want to tell their wives everything. In fact, you do not want to know everything that goes on inside your husband's mind! He can find a great deal of encouragement, healing and spiritual development by spending time with other men—especially men who are more spiritually mature.

Many men carry a great deal of emotional baggage because they did not have fathers or because their fathers were distant, uninvolved or abusive. This can create deep insecurities, fears or voids that can lead to depression, workaholism, alcoholism, sexual addictions and other problems. One of the best ways to overcome this is to link needy men with strong, emotionally mature men who can mentor and disciple them.

Your husband may not be ready to get into a Christian men's group or a one-on-one mentoring relationship. But you can make this a priority in prayer. Ask God to bring a man into your husband's life who can provide friendship and encouragement, and then wait and see what God does. Don't push your husband too fast. If there is an announcement at your church about a men's group forming, don't poke him in the ribs or manipulate him to go. Let God do the work in him.

If you feel prompted by the Holy Spirit, you might want to mention to a mature man in your church that your husband needs encouragement. But be low-key and discreet about this. Men do not enjoy being ganged up on. And if your husband feels you are conspiring to "fix" his problems, he will most likely retaliate by retreating deeper inside his shell. One of the greatest obstacles men face is the challenge to swallow male pride and become transparent about their failures and weaknesses. If they are pushed into an uncomfortable place that requires them to confess their sins, they may bolt and run in the other direction.

4. Don't let your husband hold you back from fulfilling your own spiritual calling.

You need to dismiss the idea that you cannot be more spiritual than your husband. There are plenty of women mentioned in the Bible who seemed to far outshine their spouses in character and godly wisdom. One of them, Abigail, was married to a wicked, self-absorbed man named Nabal, whom she herself described as a "fool" (1 Sam. 25:25, NIV). Instead of submitting to her husband's selfish plans, she went behind his back and did the right thing, and God blessed her. She honored God, interceded on behalf of her husband and won King David's favor with her spiritual insight and godly character. Her husband died when he learned of her righteous actions, and David ended up taking Abigail as his own wife.

Abigail certainly breaks the mold of the "submissive wife" that we tend to elevate as a standard in our modern evangelical subculture. Conservative Bible teachers who twist Scripture to suggest that women should always submit to their husbands' wishes might as well cut 1 Samuel 25 out of their Bibles. God, in fact, blessed Abigail for her lack of submission to Nabal, who showed no respect for the reign of David or God's plan for Israel. Abigail, meanwhile, was brought into the palace of David because she embraced God's agenda. Abigail's story proves that women who are married to fools can enjoy an intimate place of fellowship with God!

Whether you are married to a Nabal or to a spiritually immature man who needs encouragement and nurturing discipleship, you do not have to wait for your husband to catch up with you as you pursue God on your own. If you make your relationship with God a priority and learn to chase after Him with passion and diligence, you will be better equipped to inspire others to run with you.

Question #8
When Marriage and Ministry Collide

I sense a definite call to ministry, but my husband does not even believe women can function in ministry positions. I feel so torn. I know I must submit to him, yet I feel I am being unfaithful to God by not pursuing my calling. What should I do?

This is a complicated and potentially divisive question, but I hear it often. Each woman who struggles with this issue faces a unique set of circumstances, and I would do her a disservice if I offered a one-size-fits-all pat answer. Some women are married to non-Christian husbands. Others have Christian husbands who simply do not share their passion for ministry. Others are married to Christian men who strongly disagree on a theological basis with the idea of a woman preaching or pastoring.

The tension in these situations can be intense since the Bible calls Christians to walk in faithfulness in both our ministry callings and in our marriages. When these two collide, do we pursue our calling first and risk hurting the marriage? Do we jeopardize our relationship with our spouse in order to follow what we sense is God's leading? Do we seek to preserve the marriage at all costs, as most Christian family counselors would certainly advise? Or is it possible that a marriage relationship can actually become an idol that keeps us from serving God?

The life of Pentecostal evangelist Aimee Semple McPherson (1890–1944) is an interesting case study to consider when examining this difficult subject. Sister Aimee, as her admirers knew her, felt a strong call to gospel ministry early in life. When she married her first husband, Robert Semple, they used The Salvation Army wedding vows—which are unique because both husband and wife pledged to each other that they would never do anything "to lessen devotion to God." In their ceremony, Robert also promised to use his influence to promote Aimee's "constant and entire self-sacrifice for the salvation of the world."[1]

Robert and Aimee were happy, but after they went to China as missionaries he contracted dysentery and suddenly died. Aimee returned to the United States and soon married Harold McPherson, a Christian man who supported his wife's ambitions but did not possess the same ministry giftings as Aimee's first husband. After a short while she grew dissatisfied with trying to be a housewife and felt that she was neglecting her evangelistic calling. When she became ill and was hospitalized, she claimed that God showed her that her sickness was a result of disobedience.

> As [Aimee] told it, her condition deteriorated until hospital attendants moved her into a room set apart for the dying. She struggled to breathe, and heard a nurse say, "She's going." Then she heard another voice she believed to be the voice of God, loud and definite: "NOW . . . WILL . . . YOU . . . GO?" She sensed that it was just a matter of where she went—either into eternity or into the ministry, and she yielded. Instantly the pain was gone, her breathing eased, and within two weeks she was up and about, slowly regaining strength

... Confronted by irresistible grace and divine providence, she had been left no choice but to "go."[2]

With this unusual commissioning, Aimee packed up her belongings, along with her two small children, and headed to Canada—where she began a series of revival meetings without her husband's consent. Harold sent a steady barrage of letters and telegrams to protest her decision, but he eventually joined her in Canada, abruptly changed his attitude and began helping her organize her preaching events—which attracted huge crowds to venues all along the eastern seaboard. For two years he acted as her front man, pitching her gospel tent and securing meeting halls. But in 1918 he chose to separate from her, and they divorced quietly in 1921.

In subsequent years, after she had moved to Los Angeles and founded what is now the International Church of the Foursquare Gospel, Aimee came to view her marriage to Harold McPherson as a tragic mistake. "In her mind," says biographer Edith L. Blumhofer, "what had happened was clear: like the prophet Jonah in the Old Testament, she had attempted to run from God, and Harold had been part of that running."[3] In Pentecostal circles people defended Aimee's divorce, suggesting that she had no choice but to end the marriage. After all, she was accountable to God for many souls, yet her husband did not want her preaching. So she had to choose to follow God instead of Harold.

I am certainly not offering Aimee Semple McPherson's story as an example to follow. Hers is a most unusual case. Had she been in ministry in today's evangelical culture, she might have been sidelined for her failed marriage. But in the revival atmosphere of 1920s Pentecostalism, much more priority was placed on a person's obedience to the voice of the Spirit.

It is intriguing that the denomination that Aimee founded has emerged as one of today's fastest-growing Pentecostal bodies, particularly in Africa and Latin America. One cannot help but wonder how different the world would be if this unusual woman (who was known to preach in elaborate costumes and stage Broadway-style spectacles to attract sinners to church) had put her marriage to Harold McPherson in front of her call. It certainly seems that God's blessing remained on Aimee's ministry and movement, in spite of the fact that her husband chose not to support her. In later years, Aimee married for a third time, this time to David Hutton, who also filed for divorce after a brief marriage.

The question remains: Are there situations when following God's plan could bring disruption to a marriage or a family? The Bible certainly indicates that this will happen. Jesus Himself jeopardized His relationship with His mother and brothers when they tried to stop Him from fulfilling His ministry. He then announced that His only true mother and brothers were those who "[do] God's will" (Mark 3:35, NIV). He also warned His followers that radical discipleship can and will disrupt families:

> Do not think that I came to bring peace on the earth; I did not come to bring peace, but a sword. For I came to set a man against his father, and a daughter against her mother, and a daughter-in-law against her mother-in-law; and a man's enemies will be the members of his household.
>
> —MATTHEW 10:34–36

The apostle Paul also wrote that married people would experience more difficult problems in ministry than those who are single. Unmarried people, Paul said, are free from concern (1 Cor. 7:32), while a married man is "concerned about the things of the world, how he may please his wife, and his interests are divided" (vv. 33–34). Paul was most likely referring to the divided interests that occur when one marriage partner does not share the spiritual goals or desires of the other spouse.

When there is a conflict in a marriage caused by a spouse's ministry calling, I certainly do not believe that this should always lead to separation or divorce. In most cases, the situation provides an opportunity for both partners to grow in their relationship with God and each other as they work to resolve their differences.

What to Do If Your Spouse Will Not Support Your Ministry Calling

I would recommend that you keep the following guidelines in mind if you find yourself in this situation:

1. Don't be angry or defensive.

Be honest with your husband about your desires, and share what you feel God is saying to you. If he is hostile, or if he dismisses your sense of calling, don't allow an offense to grow in your heart. Take your situation to the Lord in prayer, and cast all your anxieties on Him. Constantly allow the Holy Spirit to check your attitudes, and, by all means, don't allow a spirit of pride or spiritual superiority to lodge in your heart. Stay humble and loving. And don't be impatient. God is not required to act according to your schedule. Let Him work sovereignly.

2. Pray for your husband.

If he is resisting God's will for your life, then God is certainly able to soften his heart. Perhaps your husband is struggling with a fear of losing control. Or perhaps he has had a negative experience with ministry that causes him to resent Christian workers in general. Ask God to touch the hidden places of your husband's heart where fear, cynicism, anger or offense resides. Also, be open to the fact that God could be using your husband's resistance to speak to you. Perhaps you are not as ready for a ministry assignment as you think you are. If your husband is a spiritual man, he may be seeing something that you don't.

3. Develop a proper attitude about submission.

Many Christian couples have been taught that the apostle Paul's words about marriage in Ephesians 5:21–33 require women to blindly obey their husbands in all situations—as if Paul were setting up some kind of hierarchy in the home with the husband on a throne. This was not Paul's intention. In fact, he never once called on women to obey their husbands, right or wrong. Such reverential obedience would actually be idolatry. His point in the passage was to reinforce the unique and intimate relationship that husbands and wives enjoy—a harmony that can be achieved through mutual submission and selfless love.

Paul told wives, "Be subject to your own husbands, *as to the Lord* (Eph. 5:22, emphasis added). In Colossians, he said, "Wives, be subject to your husbands, *as is fitting in the Lord*" (Col. 3:18, emphasis added). Charles Trombley points out that this places definite conditions on how a wife submits to her husband. "In both passages the wives' submission is to be in accordance with what is acceptable to the Lord—it is not a blanket order."[4] This means that it would actually be sinful for a woman to concede to her husband's wishes if he is asking her to do something that is outside of God's will.

4. Discern your calling properly.

If you feel called into the ministry, and your husband is resistant to your involvement in church activities, don't quickly assume that you have all the answers or that your husband is standing in your way. Trust God to intervene on your behalf and to confirm His will for your life. If your calling is from God, you will not be able to escape it, nor will your husband be able to snuff it out. Others will recognize it, and doors will be opened for you because of God's favor and blessing. This could lead to potential conflict, but you should seek to maintain peace.

5. Keep fueling the fire of personal revival.

It can be discouraging when the one person we love the most does not support our aspirations and goals. Many women who feel called to some aspect of ministry, and who don't find any encouragement from their husbands, allow their spiritual passion to wane. Don't allow your fire to die out. You have your own relationship with God—your husband is not your spiritual mediator. If your husband's lack of encouragement is enough to keep you off the spiritual battlefield, what will you do when persecution comes from others? Perhaps this is a test to see if you will remain faithful in devotion to God no matter what opposition is thrown your way.

6. Learn to embrace the fire of testing.

Author Bob Sorge, in his excellent book *The Fire of Delayed Answers,* says that one of God's most effective means of purifying our lives is to delay answers to our prayers. After enduring some difficult personal trials, Sorge realized that God often puts His people in a "prison" of circumstances or afflictions in order to test and purify us. But the outcome of this affliction, he says, is always one of hope:

> You've been persevering for weeks, or months, or possibly even years. You've known darkness, pain, perplexity and fire. You don't understand why God is allowing all this. And then one day it's as though you awaken from a sleep, and it suddenly hits you. "I'm different! God has used this trial to revolutionize me! This tribulation is none other than the love of God for me."[5]

If you find yourself in a prison of limitation, embrace the season and allow God to draw you closer to Himself. God may have imprisoned you in order to change you. When it is time for your release, let God open the door. After passing though His fires of testing, you will be ready for whatever assignment He has for you.

7. Be willing to make a difficult choice.

Many women have said to me, "I'd like to be more involved in ministry, but my husband won't let me." I am not convinced that such an excuse will be acceptable when we stand before God and give an account for our lives. Rarely would I ever counsel a woman to end her marriage because her Christian husband did not want her to fulfill her ministry call. But, by the same token, I would not tell a woman that keeping her marriage together "at all costs" was her absolute goal in life. To say that would be to put family on a higher pedestal than God.

I know an evangelist who felt called to life in the inner city. Conditions were tough on the streets, but this man and his wife carried out a fruitful ministry among drug addicts, prostitutes, homeless people and poor children. However, after a few years the evangelist's wife began to grow weary of the strains of urban life. She disliked the constant fear of violence, the smell of the streets and the people's endless need for pastoral care. She wanted to leave the ministry and find a more "normal" life in the suburbs. Her husband, meanwhile, felt he could not abandon his call to work with the poor.

As it turned out, the woman chose to leave her husband. She basically told him, "It's either me or the ministry." That is a hard choice for anyone to make. After all, most popular books about Christian marriage and family would suggest that this man should have done whatever he could to salvage his marriage. Instead, he allowed his wife to leave him. She eventually remarried, and he continued his work on the streets, knowing that he would suffer constant criticism. In the end, he felt he had to obey God's call.

Some Christians will probably always hold this man in contempt and say that he should have put his wife first. Others have defended him and blamed the wife for being selfish. Ultimately, the judgments of men don't matter. If this man was following God's call, then ultimately it will be made obvious at the judgment seat of Christ.

I hope you do not have to face a hard choice like this, but if you do, keep a humble spirit and be open to the correction and counsel of mature Christians. And remember that you too will give an account for the spiritual gifts you have been given and for the way you invested them in the kingdom during your lifetime.

Question #9
Let's Hear It for Single Women

I am a single woman, and pastors at my church have told me that I cannot serve in a leadership capacity until I am married. Is this biblical?

Policies that exclude single women from certain positions in church life are usually rooted in one of two erroneous views of Scripture. One is based on the apostle Paul's qualifications for elders in 1 Timothy 3:2–7, which include the stipulation that the man must be "the husband of one wife." Some churches use this passage to require that all elders must be male; others have used it, as well, to insist that only married men can serve in pastoral positions.

Many Bible scholars, however, believe that what Paul was actually stating was that male church leaders, who are being specifically addressed in that passage, cannot be involved in polygamy. In fact, 1 Timothy 3:2 is the first and only time in Scripture when the practice of having multiple wives is addressed.

The second erroneous view is loosely based on 1 Corinthians 11:3, which states that "the man is the head of a woman." (This verse should actually be translated, "The head of the *wife* is the *husband*.") From this passage, some traditionally minded evangelicals have derived a concept of *male covering*, which suggests that a woman who does not have a husband is *uncovered* or out from under proper authority. Thus, some churches have crafted a policy that states that an unmarried woman cannot serve in any leadership role until she is married and obtains a *head*, or *covering*.

Neither one of these Scriptures can be used as the basis for such a rule. In 1 Timothy 3, after Paul gave qualifications for male church leaders, he also listed qualifications for female leaders (v. 11). Unfortunately, some Bible translators have changed the meaning of the verse, assuming that Paul's directives were being given to "their wives" or "the wives of deacons," rather than to "women" as the Greek text clearly states.

Paul, in fact, had many women on his apostolic team, and he mentioned several women in his epistles who were either pastoring churches or active in itinerant evangelistic ministry. Of course we do not know if Phoebe, a deacon mentioned in Romans 16:1–2, was single, but we have no reason to believe that Paul would have disqualified a person from ministry because of singleness. Paul himself was single, and he advocated celibacy in some cases.

The idea that a woman must have a "male head" in order to function in an authoritative role is at best a form of Christian superstition, because it has no basis in the Bible. Paul's reference to a husband being the "head of the wife" is an allusion to the Creation story, in which Eve was taken out of Adam. Rather than establishing a chain of authority, the headship principle reminds us that husbands and wives enjoy a mystical union that is not paralleled in any other human relationship. Headship implies connection and partnership, not domination or hierarchy.

To suggest that a single woman cannot serve in the church because she does not have a "male head" is, in fact, heretical, because it implies that a man, rather than Christ alone, can give a woman spiritual authority and genuine anointing.

I can assure you that there is absolutely no scriptural reason for disqualifying a woman from Christian service because she is unmarried. The leaders of your church probably did not invent this misguided policy on their own; instead, they borrowed it from a long tradition of gender bias. They based it not on biblical truth but on a degrading view of women that values them not for their God-given individual worth as children of God, made in His image, but rather for their sexuality and their ability to reproduce. While married women in the church have suffered greatly under this oppression, single women have carried a double portion of it.

In many cultures, a woman derives her total value from her ability to have children. This idea has certainly been promoted within the church in times past. Martin Luther, the father of the Protestant Reformation, had a shockingly crass and insensitive perspective on women and marriage. He once wrote: "Take women from their housewifery, and they are good for nothing." He also believed that if women die in childbirth, "there is no harm in that; let them die as long as they bear; they are made for that."[1]

Is it any wonder that we in the church today struggle to overcome gender prejudice when revered leaders such as Luther held such blatantly sexist views? Luther's attitude was actually a carryover from ancient times. In all of the earliest civilizations—including ancient Jewish culture—women were valued for their wombs, not their minds or personalities. They were servants, sex objects and mindless baby-making machines. So naturally, if a woman could not have children or did not marry, she had no worth whatsoever. In these backward cultures, no one would dare suggest that a woman could be educated, have a profession or make any kind of valuable contribution to society.

This is why, in so many parts of the world, female infants are considered substandard and are even abandoned by their parents after birth. In India, where baby boys are prized, women are aborting their infants at an alarming rate when ultrasound imaging determines they are carrying girls. In China, where the communist government imposes a "one child per family" policy, girl infants are often aborted or killed at birth so that the family can opt for a male child. In Nigeria, a woman who gives birth to only girls is considered a reproach to her husband, and he will often be encouraged by his relatives to divorce his wife if she does not produce a son. (A strange custom indeed, since biological research has proven that it is the father's sperm that determines the sex of the child.)

When I was in Nigeria in 2002, a twenty-five-year-old single woman came to me after a church service, seeking prayer. She fought back tears as she explained that her father was divorcing her mother because she had only given him five daughters and no sons. The man had already moved to another city and was planning to marry a new, younger wife, thus ending a twenty-seven-year marriage. The man's relatives were fully supportive of his decision since they considered it disgraceful that he had no male heir.

I could not fathom the pain that this young woman was feeling. Her father's decision had serious economic implications as well, since he was not leaving any form of inheritance to his wife or his five girls. In fact, they were expected to leave the house and find a new way to support themselves. The worst part of the story is that this man was a professing Christian. He obviously believed that his decision to divorce his wife was justified. And, sadly, many churches in Nigeria would most likely support his decision because this cultural prejudice is so deeply ingrained in the society.

Nigerian law, I discovered, does not afford a wife in this situation any means to obtain justice. In essence, the society condones the cruelty of male domination. Nigerian tradition says that a woman's worth is totally linked to her attachment to a man. Without a husband or a male child, she is nothing. Maleness determines value.

After talking about this situation with several Nigerian pastors, I also discovered that widows in Nigeria face incredible oppression. If a woman's husband dies prematurely, she is often treated like a leper. Her husband's relatives often will evict her from her home, and she will be thrown in the street with no inheritance and no hope of obtaining a job. Because of superstitions rooted in witchcraft, many Nigerians believe widows are under some form of curse, so they refuse to help them.

The Bible, of course, does not teach that men are more valuable than women or that women derive their value from their attachment to a man. God does not place more value on boys than girls. Nor does He favor married people over single people. When He created the world, He chose to fill it with both men and women, and He delights in having fellowship with His children, who are valued equally in His sight. The oppression that women have suffered over the centuries was not authored by God, but rather is the result of the curse of sin, which Jesus Christ defeated. (See Genesis 3:16.)

The Value of Women

Let's examine a few passages in the Bible that make it clear that women have their own intrinsic value in the sight of God apart from their attachment to men.

1. The case of Zelophehad's daughters (Num. 27:1–11)

Zelophehad, a member of the tribe of Manasseh, had five daughters who were bold enough to approach the tent of Moses and ask for an audience with him. Their complaint was that they were going to be denied an inheritance because of their gender. They told Moses, "Give us property among our father's relatives" (v. 4, NIV). When Moses inquired of the Lord about this, God said to him, "What Zelophehad's daughters are saying is right. You must certainly give them property as an inheritance among their father's relatives and turn their father's inheritance over to them" (v. 7, NIV).

This was a revolutionary moment in the history of Israel, because what God said to Moses contradicted centuries of unjust treatment of women. The counsel that Moses received from the Lord that day became a legal precedent in Israel, overturning previous notions about women's inferiority. The counsel of the Lord was clear: Women have the same value and the same rights as their brothers.

2. God's hand on single women in the Old Testament

We have plenty of evidence that God went out of His way to anoint single women under the Old Covenant. Moses' sister, Miriam, the first worship leader in the Bible, was a prophetess who had governmental responsibilities (Mic. 6:4), yet the Scriptures never say anything about Miriam having a husband. Linda Belleville, in her book *Women Leaders and the Church*, writes:

> Miriam's ministry skills were not only recognized and confirmed, but she was accorded the same respect Aaron and Moses received. In fact, her leadership abilities were held in such high esteem that Israel would not travel until she had been restored to them (Num. 12:1–16).[2]

One of the most beautifully written parts of the Bible, the

Book of Ruth, tells the story of a young Moabite widow whose faith in the God of Israel placed her in the very lineage of Christ. While her society considered Ruth a lowly outcast because of her ancestral background and widowed status, God chose to use her life to illustrate His miraculous plan of redemption. Because of her faith, her mother-in-law, Naomi, praised her as being better "than seven sons" (Ruth 4:15).

The young maiden Esther, an orphan girl who was valued only for her beauty by a pagan king, was used by God to deliver the captive nation of Israel from genocide. Her faith, joined with the fasting and prayers of her young maidens, brought about a spiritual victory. Likewise, the faithful prayers of the prophetess Anna, an elderly widow, paved the way for the advent of the Savior. Like many other Old Testament prophets (she is referred to as a prophetess in Luke 2:36), Anna publicly called God's people to anticipate the coming of the Messiah.

3. Jesus' attitude toward single women

While the society of Jesus' day pushed women into the sidelines and shadows, causing them to suffer horribly, Jesus went out of His way to touch them, heal them and lift them out of the prison of injustice. He healed a hemorrhaging woman who had spent all of her money on doctors who couldn't help her (Mark 5:25–34). He showed compassion and extended God's forgiveness to a prostitute, even while His religious critics watched (Luke 7:36–50). He broke every rule of cultural decorum by ministering to a Samaritan divorcee who had been abused and mistreated by all the men in her life (John 4:7–26).

Jesus also had women friends, including two sisters, Mary and Martha, who were single. He had women followers on his apostolic team, and although we don't know the marital status of all of them, it is most likely that Mary Magdalene was unmarried. Jesus chose her to be the first to announce His Resurrection.

In one of the most poignant scenes in the Gospels, Jesus is moved with compassion when he meets the widow of Nain (Luke 7:11–17). Her world had just caved in because her only son had died—thus eliminating her only hope for livelihood. With her son gone, she would be pushed to the bottom rung of society and perhaps be forced to become a beggar. But when Jesus passed by the funeral, He could not ignore her grief. He raised her son to life, reminding all of Israel of the way the Old Testament prophet Elijah had once helped another desperate widow in Zarephath (Luke 4:24–26).

Obviously, Jesus had a special place in his heart for widows. He frequently used them to illustrate His parables (most writers of the day did not pay attention to women at all), and He singled out a poor widow as an example of selfless giving when she brought her two small coins to the temple treasury (Luke 21:1–4). When He told the crowd that the poor woman had "put in more than all of them" (v. 3), He was making it clear that women—even those deemed *worthless* by society—had exceptional value in the eyes of God.

In spite of the prejudices of men, single women have for centuries been used by God to serve the church and to carry the gospel around the world. If you study the history of missions, you will find that some of the greatest spiritual breakthroughs were accomplished by dedicated single women who left marriage and family behind and risked disease and death to pioneer Christ's work in China, India, Africa and even in the cold Arctic.

One of those brave single women is Kayy Gordon, who spent forty years of her life ministering to Inuit tribes in the icy regions of northern Canada. She felt a call from God to preach to these people in the 1960s, and she found little support from Christians who felt it was unseemly for a single woman to trek all by herself in the barren tundra. But with God's help, she went from village to village, taking the gospel to the Inuit people by dogsled and later by small planes.

When she retired from her work some forty years later, Kayy had planted twelve churches and two Bible colleges, and her converts—both men and women—now carry on her work. A notable Pentecostal revival has begun to sweep the region, now known as Nunavut. The seeds of this revival were sown by an unknown spinster named Kayy Gordon who did not have a "male head" and did not turn away from her calling just because some critics say women can't be evangelists or church planters.

When *Charisma* did a cover story on Kayy's work in December 2000, she told a reporter that a few Christian men had courted her. "It's true I did have others show an interest in me," Gordon said, "but I simply felt too fulfilled in life to get involved."[3]

A missionary colleague of Kayy's, Lynn Patterson, had been inspired by her example and became a pastor and administrator of one of the key Arctic missionary bases located in Yellowknife, Canada. When asked by *Charisma* if she planned to marry, Lynn had a similar response: "A husband? He'd have to be someone who had a real call of God on his life to travel to fourteen different Arctic communities," Lynn said. "I'm a lady. I will never chase a man. If God has a man for me, I'll know it."[4]

Neither of these female missionary pioneers needed a man to legitimize her ministry. I wonder what the world would be like today if all the Kayy Gordons and Lynn Pattersons of the world stayed home and waited for a *male head* to cover them? In Kayy's case, that man may never have come, and thousands of people in the Arctic would have never heard about Jesus. I wonder how many mission fields remain desolate today because single women either didn't have permission from their church leaders to go, or they didn't think God would work through their simple offering of pure-hearted faith and devotion.

Single women can be called, equipped, appointed and commissioned to do whatever the Holy Spirit directs them to do, and the church should be funding their efforts rather than putting obstacles in their way.

Question #10
Women Aren't Second-String

Someone once told me that the only time a woman can be called into the ministry is when a man refuses God's call. Is this a biblical view? Are women God's "second choice" for leadership roles?

This is certainly not a biblical view, but many women throughout church history have believed the lie that they were God's second choice. Kathryn Kuhlman, the great charismatic healing evangelist who brought widespread renewal to mainline churches in the United States during the 1950s and 1960s, was said to have believed that she was called into the ministry only because a man was running from his assignment. British missionary Gladys Aylward, whose work in China was the inspiration for a Hollywood film, believed that she was sent to the field only because a man refused to go.

This odd notion took hold in the 1800s because of the bizarre double standard that American churches and mission agencies adopted toward female ministers. Women were barred from preaching or holding pastoral positions in most denominations at the time, but if they went to the mission field, they often were thrust immediately into the rigorous work of evangelism, Bible teaching and church planting. Some male missionary leaders encouraged this trend, while others simply looked the other way and pretended to ignore it. But when these same women visited the home front, even those who had carried on public preaching ministries were told they could not even stand in the pulpit, much less address an audience.

Many women ministers of the day accepted this double standard with an awkward graciousness. One Methodist missionary to India, Isabella Thoburn, agreed to speak at a church while she was home on furlough, but only on the condition that she would speak from the front pew, not from the podium.[1] Women like Thoburn obviously felt that they were doing a "man's job" if they preached from a pulpit in a Western church, yet they felt much more comfortable doing this same task in a foreign country because they were functioning in the role a man had "refused."

When the call for missionaries began to be heard in Western churches in the mid-1800s, there is no doubt that mission agencies were surprised by the number of women who responded. Women were actually more eager to sail to primitive regions of the world—to dangerous places where married men did not want to take their wives and children because of the risk of disease. Rather than acknowledge that God was sovereignly calling both men and women to the harvest fields, church leaders rationalized that this anointed army of women was an anomaly—assembled because so few men were responding to the call. Women thus became God's glorious substitutes.

This idea was reinforced among Pentecostals in the 1920s and again in the 1940s after both world wars. Because so many men were drafted for military service, there were fewer men available to fill pulpits. This is one reason so many Pentecostal women found greater openness to preach and pastor in the 1940s. The attitude was actually quite sexist: "Since the men are all gone, you will have to fill in." Once again, women were cast as second-string players.

It all sounds ridiculous, but this strange notion still haunts many women today. Society and the church tell them that they are second class, second rate and of lesser importance than men. To overcome this fallacy we need to understand what the Bible says about our spiritual callings.

God told the prophet Jeremiah that he had been set apart from his mother's womb to be a prophet to Israel. This concept of prophetic calling from one's birth is found throughout the Bible. An angel announced to Samson's mother that she would give birth to a special son. A similar announcement came to John the Baptist's father, Zacharias. God told the young Joseph in a dream that he would be a ruler among his brothers.

King David understood that his life had been ordained by God before his birth. He wrote, "You knit me together in my mother's womb...your eyes saw my unformed body. All the days ordained for me were written in your book before one of them came to be" (Ps. 139:13, 16, NIV). This is true for each of us. We have a destiny. God does not simply throw us into the world to see what we will do; He fills us with a sense of prophetic mission. The apostle Paul taught that God predestines His plans and purposes for us (Eph. 1:11–12), and then he prayed for the Ephesian believers that they might, with spiritual insight, "know the hope to which he has called you" (v. 18, NIV). Paul then explained that each of us, as believers, has been created with a special purpose:

> For we are His workmanship, created in Christ Jesus for good works, *which God prepared beforehand,* that we should walk in them.
>
> —EPHESIANS 2:10, EMPHASIS ADDED

If this is true, then obviously men *and* women are called by God from birth for specific assignments. Nowhere in the Bible are we told that if we don't fulfill our assignment, God gives it to someone else. In the story of Jonah, for example, God became angry with Jonah when he shirked from his calling, and the reluctant prophet's three days and nights inside the fish taught him that running from God is not a wise choice.

Heaven's assignments are not just given to men, either. The female prophets of the Old Testament, such as Huldah and Deborah, obviously spoke from inspiration and carried with them a sense of divine calling. When the Lord initiated His covenant with Abram and changed his name to Abraham, He included Sarai in the promise and spoke of her prophetic mission. God said, "As for Sarai your wife, you shall not call her name Sarai, but Sarah shall be her name. And I will bless her, and indeed I will give you a son by her. Then I will bless her, and she shall be a mother of nations; kings of peoples shall come from her" (Gen. 17:15–16).

When Hannah gave birth to Samuel and sent him to the priest Eli to be raised in the temple, she launched into a song of praise to God that celebrates her special calling. Deborah sang a similar song in Judges 5, in which she praises the Lord for the fact that He used her to rally Israel in war to defeat Sisera's army. Deborah understood her calling as a leader in Israel, and she knew by divine insight where she fit in the grand scheme of God's eternal purpose. The Virgin Mary obviously had this same sense of destiny after she became pregnant with the Messiah. She sang out: "From this time on all generations will count me blessed. For the Mighty One has done great things for me; and holy is His name" (Luke 1:48–49).

Yet there is one Bible character who best illustrates the fact that

God can and does call women to special tasks. Her name was Esther, and a whole book of the Old Testament is devoted to her dramatic story—one that reminds us that God's best weapon is often a woman.

We don't know what was going on in Esther's mind when she was a young girl, or whether she had any special sense of calling or destiny. We do know that her parents had died when she was young, and that her older cousin, Mordecai, had adopted her as his own daughter. Mordecai was a godly man, and it is likely that he had been given insight from God about this special young girl. Perhaps he sensed that she had been preserved for a holy task.

That task became clearer when this Jewish maiden was confiscated from her home by palace guards and ordered to audition for the harem of King Xerxes. When Mordecai learned that the king was being tricked into ordering the genocide of all Jews, he realized that even though Esther had been placed in a dangerous and compromising position, it was God who had put her there for His own purpose. She would be the instrument God would use to deliver His people.

Mordecai unveiled the enemy's evil plot and then instructed Esther to intervene by speaking to the king. Her mission was accompanied by incredible risk, but Mordecai told her, "Who knows whether you have not attained royalty for such a time as this?" (Esther 4:14).

Esther's intervention, of course, saved a nation. Yet the Bible never tells us that she was God's second choice for this assignment or that a man would have done a better job. No, God had fashioned her "from the foundation of the world" to speak on behalf of God's people. Just like Moses—who also was destined from birth to grow up in the house of Pharaoh and to liberate God's people from Egyptian bondage—Esther was marked as God's messenger.

She was not God's second choice, and neither are you. Like Esther, your obedience to a heavenly calling could result in the spiritual liberation of thousands. Don't wait for a man to send you. Don't wait for a man to legitimize you. You've been called "for such a time as this."

Question #11
Role-Playing and
Other Dumb Games

I'm discouraged because there are so few opportunities for ministry at my church. Most positions are for men only, and I don't feel particularly gifted to do children's ministry. What should I do?

Conservative evangelical churches have developed some odd ideas about what men and women can do in ministry. It is assumed that only a man can lead (since he is the "head") and that only men should teach Scripture to mixed groups. So the men are drafted to head committees, spearhead outreach projects or teach classes, even though qualified women are usually available and willing to serve. At the same time, women are exhorted to fill support roles when it may actually be a man who is more gifted to serve in those functions.

All of this typecasting is based on a nebulous idea of biblical "roles" for men and women. Although such roles are not defined in Scripture, the traditions have been passed down from previous generations of churchgoers and then upheld by traditionalists in our seminaries. Today these traditionalists warn us that if we allow women to teach the Bible or pastor a church, this will destroy the "biblical role of women" and thus lead all of us into heresy and cultural depravity. Meanwhile, they say, the institution of the family will be annihilated because women are abandoning the home to pursue goals or careers that are not within this feminine "role."

Let's not forget that Christians in the United States used these same arguments in the late 1890s and early 1900s to try to stop women from gaining the right to vote. In a pamphlet called *Woman Suffrage,* conservative preacher John Milton Williams, in 1893, claimed that woman was "the divinely appointed guardian of the home." He claimed that because of this responsibility, woman "has no call to the ballot box."[1] Roman Catholic bishops in Massachusetts apparently agreed with Williams, because they voted in 1920 that a woman who entered the political sphere was a "fallen woman."[2] Other conservative churches in that time period also passed resolutions opposing women's suffrage.

In 1920, one fundamentalist Christian newspaper chastised women for entering the work force, warning that the nation would break down as a result. "The distinctive function and the supreme mission of woman is home-making," the *Watchman-Examiner* said.[3] Other conservative religious voices opposed the women's suffrage movement on the grounds that social reform movements were not necessary because the return of Jesus Christ was imminent.

So what is the "biblical role" of a woman? This is an odd question indeed, since women in the Bible carried out all kinds of diverse assignments. They were prophets, entrepreneurs, queens, servants, slaves, deacons, midwives, mothers, teachers, singers, dancers, evangelists, messengers . . . the list could go on. It would be difficult to draw lines of limitation and say that women must be one thing or another. The Bible, in fact, says that every person is created in God's image with unique and special gifts and callings. Why would we want to limit any person to a particular "role"?

Not all women are married, nor are all women mothers. Therefore it is especially odd that the church has told women for centuries that their "role" is to guard the home and raise children. And just because women have children, does this mean raising them is their only assignment in life? We certainly do not say that about men who are fathers.

We need to admit that the whole argument about roles is a clever religious way to candy-coat chauvinism and pride. What we are really implying, when we define this so-called woman's role, is that God doesn't want her to assume "a man's role."

And what is a man's "biblical role"? Again, traditionalists define this narrowly by saying that man is called to lead his family and the church. But again, let's look at men in the Bible. Were all men leaders? No—they too had all kinds of assignments. They were apostles, farmers, shepherds, warriors, priests, kings, prophets, physicians, scribes, scholars, poets, musicians and artisans. Some were married and some weren't. Some had great responsibilities; others carried no titles and governed nothing.

Of course, Scripture requires men to be men, and women to be women. God does not endorse androgyny, homosexuality or any form of gender bending. God is glorified when men act masculine and women act feminine.

But a woman does not have to have children to be feminine. Nor does a man have to be a leader in order to be masculine. I know some very godly, masculine Christian men who work in service jobs where they have no authority over other employees. And I know many Christian women who are models of feminine grace, yet they pastor churches with more than a thousand members.

A man who works as a janitor does not become effeminate simply because he does not have authority over someone else. By the same token, a woman who cares for a congregation and preaches from a pulpit every week does not take on masculine mannerisms or slowly begin morphing into a man.

Gender Myths in the Church

The assumption that "men always lead and women always follow" has created an odd and dysfunctional set of myths in the church. Some of these myths include:

1. Women are more suited to do children's ministry.

That's ridiculous, because men often are gifted with the ability to communicate the gospel to children. Just because women care for babies or young children at home does not mean they particularly want to spend their Sunday mornings in the church nursery. Yet we typically pigeonhole them for this role.

Jesus, as a man, related well to children—and He rebuked His disciples for minimizing children's importance in the kingdom. We would never say that women are better at parenting than men are—because it takes a mother and a father to make a good set of parents. For the same reason we need men and women ministering to children.

2. Women are more suited for prayer ministry.

This is a totally unbiblical notion, but many pastors promote the idea that "women pray better" because they do not allow women to do anything else. The Bible certainly does not segregate the prayer meeting by gender.

Yes, there are plenty of examples of powerful women intercessors in the Bible—such as Hannah or Anna. Conservative church leaders love to applaud these female prayer warriors as great biblical examples for women today, yet they conveniently fail to mention other biblical heroines like Deborah or Miriam who held senior governing positions. Meanwhile, men are rarely exhorted to emulate the prayer lives of male intercessors like Daniel, when God certainly does call some men to live hidden lives of devotion.

3. A woman's most valuable ministry is that of a mother.

While this statement certainly sounds laudable (who wants to minimize the impact of a mother's love?), there is often an attitude lurking behind it. That attitude says, "A woman's role is home with the kids—that's what she was created to do, and nothing else."

That doesn't do much for a single woman, except to suggest that the only way she can have value to God and the church is to get married and have babies of her own. It doesn't do much for the woman who doesn't have children, either. And what does it do for the woman whose children are grown? Is she now supposed to throw all her energy into her grandchildren?

4. Women are better suited in support roles.

The traditional religious model says the church can hire women to be secretaries, administrative assistants and receptionists. Females need not apply for ministerial positions that give them authority in the congregation. Again, that's unbiblical (as we have stated throughout this book) because we have examples of women in the Bible who were given substantial ecclesiastical authority.

And the Scripture does not say that the gift of leadership, mentioned in Romans 12:8, is given exclusively to males. Nor does it state that any of the offices in the fivefold ministry mentioned in Ephesians 4:11 (apostle, prophet, pastor, teacher and evangelist) are for men only. In fact, Paul specifically gives us character requirements for women who serve in ministry. (See 1 Timothy 3:11; Titus 2:3–5.)

5. Women are never called to lead worship.

Despite the fact that the first worship leader in the Bible was a woman (Miriam), conservative churches rarely empower women to serve in this position. Does this mean women don't have the same level of musical talent? Does it mean they cannot handle the pressure of being in front of a crowd? Some traditionalists would argue that a woman shouldn't lead worship because by doing so she is being placed in a "position of authority" over men. How ridiculous! Is she beating the men with a whip in order to make them sing?

One woman I know was told she could lead worship in an interim capacity at her church, but she was asked to do it from the floor of the auditorium rather than from the pulpit! Such bizarre policies are more rooted in fleshly religious tradition than in any biblical principle.

One conservative denomination in the United States forbids women from being worship leaders, yet their hymnal is full of the classic songs of Fannie Crosby (1820–1915), the blind musician who wrote more than a thousand hymns, including "Blessed Assurance," "Draw Me Nearer" and "All the Way My Savior Leads Me." Why would it be acceptable for her to write the hymns we sing but not to sing them in front of the church?

Darlene Zschech, a worship leader and prolific songwriter from Hillsong Church in Melbourne, Australia, has composed dozens of praise choruses that are now sung in churches around the world. Many conservative churches today will sing Darlene's most famous anthem, "Shout to the Lord," but they would never allow her to lead the song from the pulpit because of this sexist policy. Meanwhile, how many gifted female worship leaders have been ignored for positions because this is not a "woman's role"?

6. Women can never teach the Bible if there are men in the group.

We will examine this mind-set in detail in chapters eighteen and twenty. Despite the fact that there are biblical examples of women in senior positions of authority (Deborah in Judges 4), as well as instances of women instructing men (Proverbs 8; Priscilla in Acts 18:26), religious traditions die slowly. It may take another generation before we rid the church of this crippling spirit of gender prejudice—an attitude that continues to slow the advancement of the gospel.

But there are certainly signs that things are changing. It is becoming increasingly difficult for traditionalists to ignore the anointing that is on prominent female preachers, pastors and Bible teachers today—because they are becoming louder and because men are listening. Many of these women, including Beth Moore, Joyce Meyer, Juanita Bynum, Stormie Omartian, Anne Graham Lotz and Becky Tirabassi, have television programs, Bible study courses and best-selling books in the United States. Their influence can't be denied, and they are not going away.

Indeed, anointed women are arising in the global church—in Europe, Africa, Asia and South America. They are breaking all the antiquated religious rules and debunking all the myths by their example. It is time that we bless them and acknowledge that they have been commissioned and empowered to represent Christ in this generation.

Question #12
Dare to Be a Pioneer

Does the Bible say that women should always let men initiate things? I've been told that women who lead churches or start ministries are rebellious. This has prevented me from taking an initiative in ministry.

There is an unwritten rule in many churches today that says men should always *lead the way.* Because of this notion, women who attempt to lead are viewed with suspicion, and they are urged to put their spiritual ambitions on a shelf. The underlying assumption is that since man was created first and was made the "head of the woman," he always goes first.

That may sound like a convincing theory, but it has no basis in Scripture. God doesn't always go to a man first when He wants to start something. There are plenty of examples in the Bible when God called on women to accomplish His will.

The Hebrew midwives, Shiphrah and Puah, took matters into their own hands and disobeyed Pharaoh's edict when he ordered them to kill the infant sons of the Israelites (Exod. 1:15–21). The five daughters of Zelophehad bucked the patriarchal system of their day by appealing to Moses and asking for property and inheritance rights—at a time when women were denied this (Num. 27:1–11). And Moses ruled in their favor, giving women more freedom in primitive Israel.

The prophet Deborah was single-handedly responsible for rallying the tribes of Israel to volunteer for battle against the Canaanites (Judg. 4), and her valor inspired the courage that led to an impressive victory. The maiden Jael, inspired by Deborah's example, worked up the nerve to kill Sisera, the leader of the Canaanites, while he slept. Deborah's prophetic zeal and Jael's cunning bravery played strategic roles in Israel's military triumph.

When God decided to announce the birth of Samson, He sent His angel not to the child's father, Manoah, but to his mother (Judg. 13). In fact, when Manoah expressed doubt concerning the angel's instructions, the angel returned—again to Manoah's wife! She apparently had more faith and spiritual insight than her husband did.

Hannah refused to be discouraged by Eli the priest, who ridiculed her for praying so passionately. Eli, in fact, was clueless about what was happening with Hannah; he did not discern that the Holy Spirit was birthing in her a deep burden for the spiritual restoration of her nation. Hannah's burden was rewarded when God gave her a promised son who would be a prophet to the nation.

Esther risked her life to develop a plan to deliver her people from genocide. Although her cousin Mordecai supported her from outside the palace walls, only she and her female servants could carry out heaven's assignment. It is obvious that women are sometimes God's first choice.

In the New Testament, God's ultimate plan for the redemption of the world was revealed to a young girl, Mary, who was chosen to bear the Savior. God did not send the annunciation angel to

Joseph first to get his permission. Joseph had no choice in the matter, and he probably would have broken his betrothal to Mary if God had not later given him detailed instructions in a dream.

Gretchen Gaebelein Hull, in her book *Equal to Serve,* points out that Mary's role in the plan of salvation dismantles the foolish idea that women never take the lead:

> I have gone to seminars where I heard that as a woman I could make no decisions independently of my husband, father or pastor, because all women must have some sort of male authority figure in their lives to whom they are accountable. I have also heard Christian speakers say that a husband, father or pastor can negate a vow a woman has made to the Lord or overrule a decision she has made about Christian service.
>
> But if God had wanted to use a "chain of command," He would have sent Mary's call through Joseph or her father or a synagogue leader. However, inescapably, God's angelic messenger spoke to Mary directly. Therefore the Bible's own record of Mary's life contradicts such teachings.[1]

Mary had to stand alone during this unusual season in her life. Hull suggests that Mary probably did not have the full support of her own parents after she became pregnant. It is likely that they couldn't handle the stigma of keeping an unmarried pregnant girl in their home, and this would explain why Mary was sent to live with her cousin Elizabeth. (Elizabeth, in a similar way, had to stand alone. She understood God's plan more clearly than her husband, Zacharias, who was such a doubter that he was struck mute until John the Baptist was born.)

Paul the Apostle certainly dispelled the idea that women are only "followers." In fact, in his often-quoted passage about male "headship," he stated clearly that women are also initiators (1 Cor. 11:3–16). He wrote in 1 Corinthians 11:11–12:

> However, in the Lord, neither is woman independent of man, nor is man independent of woman. For as the woman originates from the man, so also the man has his birth through the woman; and all things originate from God.

Prior to these verses, Paul addressed the Corinthian leaders with questions about whether a woman should wear a veil or headdress when she prays or prophesies in church. The Corinthian elders most likely were attempting to silence the women in their assemblies, basing their actions on the fact that Adam was God's primary creation. But Paul completely dismissed this argument.

While Paul agreed that man is indeed "head of a woman" (v. 3), meaning that Adam was created first and that Eve originated from his side, the apostle said this does not give the Corinthians any basis to silence women or limit their participation in spiritual life whatsoever. Bible scholar Gilbert Bilezikian, who calls verses 11 and 12 a "sweeping disclaimer," suggests that we could paraphrase this passage in this way:

> Regardless of what may have been said or taught prior to this, in the Lord, that is, within the unity that exists among Christians, women may not be viewed apart from man, nor man from woman. For just as woman was originally made from man, now man is made with the mediation of woman. So, it all evens out. There is only one who has original primacy, and that one is God, the real source of all things (including both man and woman).[2]

The Scripture could not be clearer! Paul said men should not use their "headship" (their primacy in creation order) in any way to claim superiority over women or independence from them. Yet this is exactly what conservative evangelicals are guilty of doing! We argue that men should always "go first" and "lead the way" because "Adam was created first." Why is it that we keep harping on headship while ignoring the apostolic ultimatum in this passage?

What men in the church should be doing is exhorting women to take risks, step out in faith and set ambitious goals for ministry. We should be prodding them on. We should be opening doors for them—and gently pushing them to embrace new opportunities. So much new territory could be taken for Christ's kingdom if our women were not so conditioned to wait for men to take the first step.

And when women do take risks and show initiative, men in the church should not be threatened. We should applaud them! And we certainly have no business labeling them "rebellious" because they obeyed the promptings of His Spirit or dared to fulfill the Great Commission.

Women who are assuming leadership roles, planting churches or starting new ministries are not rebels. In fact, the true rebellious women are those who reject the Lord's voice when He calls them out of their timidity and seclusion. Some smug, self-righteous women say to God, "I can't do what you are asking me because it's not acceptable for a woman to lead." These are the women who are operating in a rebellious spirit.

Women Motivators

I am grateful today that so many women are rejecting the unhealthy religious mind-sets that have been set up like roadblocks by Satan himself. In my years as editor of *Charisma* magazine, I have met and written about literally hundreds of women who are using their creativity and spiritual gifts to pastor churches, start orphanages, launch evangelistic outreaches and even claim whole nations for Christ. Often their zeal and tenacity have motivated me, as a man, to pursue God more faithfully. These women don't intimidate me—they inspire me!

Jackie Holland—Dallas, Texas

Jackie Holland certainly wasn't going to wait for a man to lead the way. All the men in her life had been abusive. In fact, she shot one of her husbands after she discovered he had committed adultery. Miraculously he did not press charges. But the heartache of her four failed marriages eventually brought her to faith in Jesus.

When I met Jackie in 1999, years after her conversion, she had decided to let God use the garbage of her life to reach other women. She started a food pantry in a poor area of Dallas, and that ministry eventually led her to begin an outreach to strippers and prostitutes. Jackie has been a lifeline for many women who were looking for a way out of the adult entertainment business. When I last spoke with her, she was raising funds to buy a bankrupt nursing home facility. She plans to turn it into a shelter for battered women. How desperately we need more women like Jackie to feel God's heartbeat for people who have been abused and mistreated.[3]

Danita Estrella—Haiti

Danita Estrella wasn't expecting God to call her into full-time missions work when she suddenly felt the tug in the late 1990s during a visit to Haiti. When she saw some waiflike children hunting for food in a garbage dump and witnessed a man beating a child with a whip in the street, her heart broke. Single-handedly, Danita launched the Hope for Haiti orphanage with little more than compassion and some money from friends.

Today, this former promotional model is a mother to dozens of Haitian children—some of whom are HIV-positive. She purchased a building, started a school and even launched a church for the impoverished community where she now makes her home. Today, whenever she speaks, people "adopt" her Haitian orphans by pledging to support them financially.[4]

Diane Dunne—New York

It's a good thing Pastor Diane Dunne did not wait for a man to lead the way, because none of the male pastors she knows in New York City have been willing to assist her with her unusual outreach to the homeless. On Wednesday afternoons, about three hundred homeless people gather at the corner of Avenue C and Ninth Street in Manhattan's Lower East Side to receive free hot dogs, groceries and a sermon from this spunky woman preacher with a thick Brooklyn accent.[5]

"I live by faith," she told *Charisma*. "Doors don't open to speak or to raise money because I'm a woman. If you're a woman, you've got to work twice as hard in the body of Christ." Dunne, a former cosmetics company executive, quit her career and moved forty-one times while scrimping to save money for a home. She has sacrificed everything to serve Jesus among the poor. Should we stop her because she didn't wait for a man to start this ministry?

Suzette Hattingh—Germany

South African evangelist Suzette Hattingh never imagined that God would one day send her to what she considered a missionary's graveyard—Western Europe. But today she bases her ministry, called Voice in the City, in Frankfurt, Germany. In 2001 she conducted a citywide campaign in Deggendorf that energized struggling churches and led hundreds of people to first-time conversions. "Europe is dry, but I believe that there is no such thing as a country you cannot reach," she says.

Fortunately for Hattingh, she had the support of a man—German evangelist Reinhard Bonnke. He employed her on his staff for years as his prayer coordinator, but he says God told him in 1997 to "let Suzette fly like an eagle." If only more church leaders today were as willing to let women launch out on their own.[6]

Cathi Mooney—San Francisco

Few men I know are as daring as Cathi Mooney. A former advertising agency whiz, she traded her business suits and salon hairstyles to wear tie-dyed T-shirts, jeans and dreadlocks so she could reach the homeless hippies and "Deadheads" of San Francisco's Haight-Asbury district. In 1993 Cathi launched The Pioneer Project to give the gospel, warm beds and free drug counseling to some of the two thousand kids who sleep on the city's streets every night.

Not content with her ministry base in a three-story Victorian house on Asbury Street, Mooney is now planting other evangelistic outposts to reach hippie travelers overseas. One of her burdens is to evangelize the many Israeli hippies who travel to Nepal searching for a spiritual high.[7]

All of these women have one thing in common: God gave them a vision, and they pursued it with faith. None of them had extraordinary support from men. In fact, some of them have experienced opposition from men and have stood strong without taking offense. These women deserve our full support, as do so many others who have not yet stepped out to fulfill their destiny. What an army of women we could release today—if the church would discard silly notions about headship that cripple our efforts to evangelize the world.

Question #13
Strong Men, Weak Women

I don't think God equipped women with the same spiritual gifts as men. After all, the Bible says women are the "weaker vessel." Why should they be expected to lead when the New Testament says they are supposed to be "gentle" and "quiet"?

Traditionalists love to quote one particular Bible verse about woman being the "weaker vessel" to make a case for limiting women's spiritual influence or impact. It is assumed that since women are normally not as muscular as men, and because their bodies are designed to bear children and nurse them, that this somehow disqualifies them from leading, teaching Scripture or assuming spiritual responsibility. What is implied is that masculine strength qualifies a person for leadership.

This is certainly what the ancient philosophers believed. They embraced all kinds of odd conclusions about women based on their negative views of women's bodies. The Alexandrian philosopher Philo, for example, taught that because women were soft to the touch, this meant that she "easily gives way and is taken in by plausible falsehoods which resemble the truth."[1]

The Greek philosopher Aristotle wrote that women are

"defective by nature" because of biology. He believed this because women "cannot produce semen which contains a full human being."[2] Obviously Aristotle and his Greek colleagues did not understand the science of reproduction too well. He also thought that woman's inferiority was due to that fact that she lacked the body heat necessary to "cook" her menstrual fluid to the point that it would become semen![3]

Meanwhile, Plato taught that women were not completely human because they lacked masculine characteristics. "It is only males who are created directly by the gods and are given souls," he wrote.[4] Such degrading ideas, rooted in paganism, unfortunately were carried on by the fathers of the early Christian church. St. Augustine carried Greek philosophy to its natural conclusion and taught that women were not created in God's image. Another revered church father, Clement of Alexandria, believed that what made man superior was his beard and body hair. He wrote:

> By God's decree, hairiness is one of man's conspicuous qualities, and, at that, is distributed over his whole body. For what is hairy is by nature drier and warmer than what is bare; therefore, the male is hairier and more warm-blooded than the female; the uncastrated, than the castrated; the mature, than the immature.[5]

All of this is foolishness. There is absolutely nothing in the Bible that says males are superior to females or that a person's value is determined by whether they have a penis, muscular strength or body hair. What is most tragic is that such bizarre pagan ideas were embraced by the leaders of the church in the third and fourth centuries and then passed down to some of the most oft-quoted leaders of the Reformation period, including Martin Luther, John Calvin and John Knox. All of these men promoted sexist views that have more in common with the spiritual darkness of ancient Greece and

Rome than with Christianity. And yet the writings and theological views of the reformers continue to shape our seminaries today. It is no wonder that our churches are still plagued by gender prejudice.

In addition to this offensive view of women's bodies, ancient philosophers as well as early church leaders viewed women as intellectually, emotionally and morally weak. Women were type-cast as stupid, irrational, easily deceived, untrustworthy, unteach-able and sexually uncontrollable. Therefore they were cloistered indoors, denied civil rights, treated like slaves and denied educa-tional opportunities (which of course kept them ignorant). Such views have been used throughout history to keep women from gaining the right to vote, own property and attend college. The same arguments are still used to keep women out of the ministry.

This became real to me a few years ago when I asked a promi-nent theologian at a respected seminary to review something I had written about women pastors. I knew this man did not believe women should hold pastoral office, but I wanted to know exactly what scripture he based his views on. I was shocked to discover that he did not base his theology on a scripture at all, but rather on his own extra-biblical theory that "women are intellectually weaker than men and therefore are not able to teach doctrine."

This man is a respected leader in academia! Yet he holds to a medieval superstition that says women are intellectually handi-capped. (People in the 1800s used to say the same thing about African slaves until those same slaves were freed, were taught to read, went to college and became scientists, inventors, educators, social reformers, lawyers and government officials.)

Traditionalists often like to quote two passages in the apostle Peter's first epistle to support the idea that women are weak. Let's examine both of these verses. The first one is addressed to women:

And let not your adornment be merely external—

braiding the hair, and wearing gold jewelry, or putting
on dresses; but let it be the hidden person of the
heart, *with the imperishable quality of a gentle and
quiet spirit,* which is precious in the sight of God.

—1 PETER 3:3–4, EMPHASIS ADDED

The second passage is addressed to husbands:

You husbands likewise, live with your wives in an
understanding way, *as with a weaker vessel, since she is
a woman;* and grant her honor as a fellow heir of the
grace of life, so that your prayers may not be hindered.

—1 PETER 3:7, EMPHASIS ADDED

The first passage exhorts women to be modest rather than sexually provocative. When Peter asks them to exhibit "a gentle and quiet spirit," he is calling them to respectable behavior rather than to the flamboyance of prostitutes—who were known in those days to braid their hair with elaborate beads and shells and to wear ostentatious costumes in order to entice their customers. Here, Peter is simply calling women to live virtuous lives of purity and Christian character.

Yet many traditionalists have used this verse to suggest that women who are not quiet are not feminine, as if silence is a feminine virtue. On the contrary, silence can actually be sin in many situations! First Peter 3:4 does not give women the right to be quiet when they are called on to give a defense of the gospel or when they must cry out against injustice. Women who followed Christ were commissioned to "go into all the world" to preach (Mark 16:15), and the same commission has been given to women today.

The silence of women in our churches today is sin. Women who have embraced traditional teachings about "female roles" and have assumed that they are being virtuous as a result of their quietness will be surprised when they stand before the Judgment Seat of Christ to give an account for the way that they squandered their talents and spiritual gifts. God expects women to speak. He calls some of them to preach. He calls others to lift their voices like a trumpet in defense of the helpless. He calls many to teach the Bible, evangelize sinners and confront institutionalized evil. No woman can use 1 Peter 3:4 as an excuse for inaction or passivity.

Likewise, neither men nor women can use the "weaker vessel" passage, 1 Peter 3:7, to limit the fitness of women for ministry. Why is woman described as the weaker vessel? It is because she is at a disadvantage, not so much because she is weaker in a physical sense but because she has been oppressed and preyed upon by men. The curse of Genesis 3:16 has put women in a vulnerable place, but Peter instructs husbands to treat their wives with respect and honor—thereby reversing that curse.

We cannot use 1 Peter 3:7 as a proof text to claim that women are inferior to men, even in a physical sense—and certainly not in an emotional, intellectual or moral sense. It is true that most women are not built to lift heavy objects, bench press three hundred fifty pounds or play championship football. But this does not mean women have a harder time than men do when withstanding stress, resisting temptation or enduring pain. (Women, in fact, endure much more pain than most men do because of childbirth.) And medical studies today indicate that while women face a myriad of health challenges, they tend to live longer than men do.

The fact is that God has chosen to use both male and female vessels to accomplish His purposes. Those vessels are fashioned differently, yes. But the power of the Holy Spirit can flow through both. The apostle Paul, in fact, made it clear that we must never trust in the human vessel, but rather in the power of God that works inside a person. He told the Corinthians that he was in a state of "weakness and in fear and in much trembling" when he preached to them, because God would not allow him to trust in his own wisdom (1 Cor. 2:3). This was so that the faith of the Corinthians "should not rest on the wisdom of men, but on the power of God" (v. 5).

If we claim that God's power can only flow through a man, presumably because he is "stronger," then what we are really doing is trusting in flesh. Doesn't Scripture often recount for us moments in history when the weaker person—empowered by God's Spirit—overcame the stronger obstacle? David felled Goliath not because he had such a powerful arm but because God's power guided the stone. Gideon's army overcame the Midianites not because they had superior weaponry but because unseen angels routed the enemy's forces.

When wicked Abimelech was terrorizing Israel with his treachery, it was an unnamed woman who threw a millstone from the roof of a tower and crushed his skull (Judg. 9:53). Full of male pride, the wounded Abimelech asked his armor bearer to pierce him with a sword so that it could not be said that a woman killed him.

We should ponder the implications of that story. She is only identified in the Bible as "a certain woman," but this lady was God's secret weapon. She may not have been a commander in the army, but she had enough strength to toss an upper millstone from the roof and end the regime of a tyrant who had led Israel into idolatry.

How many spiritual victories have alluded us today because we did not recognize the value of the "certain women" around us? How many Abimelechs could have been defeated if we had cheered these women on—rather than telling them that God created them to be weak and passive?

Throughout the centuries, Christian women have given their

lives as martyrs for the cause of the gospel. They have been burned at the stake, torn to shreds by wild animals, had their tongues ripped out, endured rape and sexual mutilation and been left to rot in dungeons. Courageous missionary women have sailed to foreign lands and risked disease and death while ministering amid hostile tribes. Today, brave Christian women in the Middle East are being tortured with acid or electric shocks when local Muslims learn that they have been sharing their faith.

These women are heroes. In light of their testimony, do we dare suggest that women should be weak? Instead of misusing 1 Peter 3:7, we should be inspiring our sisters to be strong in the Lord. The Holy Spirit who dwells within them can and will empower them to do exploits.

They can take courage from the example of Valentina Savelieva, a Russian Baptist woman who shared her faith continually while she was moved from one Soviet prison camp to the next during the 1980s. She wrote of her experience:

> We had to keep our coats on all night because it was so cold—the temperature was seldom above 41 degrees [Fahrenheit]... When we awakened in the morning, we had to be careful not to rise too quickly, for our hair was frozen to the dirt. It was impossible to remain free from lice. Everyone was sick, and many died from tuberculosis. Food was scarce and hardly edible, and often our food was stolen. The prison was full of demon-possessed criminals, who cursed day and night. They wanted to destroy my faith.[6]

Is this the testimony of a weak woman? Valentina's unshakable faith endured long after the Soviet empire crumbled and Christians in Russia were given freedom to preach the gospel openly. Today, because of the strength of women like Valentina, a new army of

Russian women has arisen to claim their nation for Christ. One of those women is Natasha Shredrevaya, the first woman in Russia to be elected by her male peers to lead a denomination.

As president of the Calvary Fellowship of Churches of Russia, Natasha oversees thirty churches in that country and another three hundred in other former Soviet republics. Her ambitious goal is to reach the thirty-six thousand remote villages in the former USSR, a vast region that covers eight time zones. Would we deny her this opportunity because she is "too weak"? If so, what strong, better-equipped men are volunteering to take her place?

The hour is short, and we don't have time to play childish games—as if men and women in Christian ministry must compete for opportunities. There is plenty of work to do, and we need every one of our sisters working alongside their brothers in the harvest.

Their weakness is not the issue. The real question is whether both men and women in the church will learn to trade our inherent human weakness for His divine strength.

Question #14
What Do We Do With Deborah?

What do we do with Deborah in the Bible? She held a position of senior authority, but I've heard pastors say that her story can't be used to defend women in leadership.

The Old Testament most certainly allows for women in positions of authority. We've already mentioned two other female prophets in the Old Testament, Miriam and Huldah. Traditionalists who attempt to ignore or redefine the ministry of the prophet Deborah (detailed in Judges 4–5) are guilty of manipulating the text to their own advantage. They might as well take a pair of scissors and snip the Book of Judges out of the Bible.

God ordained Deborah as His mouthpiece to Israel during a forty-year period. She served as a civil and spiritual leader in much the same way that the prophet Samuel did years later. Her leadership and her sensitivity to the guidance of heaven ushered Israel into a period of peace and prosperity.

Deborah's name means "bee," perhaps a reminder that even in the insect kingdom God has set an example of female leadership. Although she was married to a man named Lappidoth, the Bible makes no mention of his involvement in his wife's role as a judge. She describes herself as "a mother in Israel" (Judg. 5:7), a reference to her governmental office. (Nineteenth-century Bible scholar Katherine Bushnell points out that the Hebrew word for "mother of Israel" here can be translated "female chief."[1])

The fact that she called herself a mother also makes it clear that although she held a position of senior authority, she was not trying to be a man, nor did she carry out her duties in a masculine way. She was not blurring gender distinctions. God had placed her in this key position. She was a mother, but mothers can rule.

Judges 4:5 tells us that "the sons of Israel came up to her for judgment," indicating that she was gifted with the supernatural wisdom and insight necessary to resolve disputes and uphold justice. She also had overwhelming trust in a transcendent God who, in response to her prophetic prayers for Israel's defense, "march[ed] from the field of Edom" (Judg. 5:4) to subdue Israel's foreign invaders.

As the story goes, Deborah summoned Israel's chief warrior, Barak, and gave him prophetic instructions on how he would subdue the Canaanites and their warlord, Sisera. Then Barak made a curious comment: "If you will go with me, then I will go; but if you will not go with me, I will not go" (Judg. 4:8). Deborah agreed to accompany the Israelite troops into the fray, but she uttered a curious prophecy before they departed.

> I will surely go with you; nevertheless, the honor shall
> not be yours on the journey that you are about to take,
> for the LORD will sell Sisera into the hands of a woman.
> —JUDGES 4:9

Many conservative Bible teachers have turned Deborah's story upside down, twisting it and rendering it useless. In their book

Recovering Biblical Manhood and Womanhood, evangelical scholars Wayne Grudem and John Piper suggest that the real purpose of Deborah's story is to bring "a living indictment of the weakness of Barak and other men in Israel who should have been more courageous leaders."[2] They suggest that Deborah broke tradition and exerted her female authority simply because the men were afraid.

This is a curious interpretation indeed, considering the fact that Barak is listed in the classic "heroes of faith" chapter—Hebrews 11. His name is recorded alongside the names of Joshua, Samson, Jephthah, David and Samuel, men who "by faith conquered kingdoms" (v. 33) and "put foreign armies to flight" (v. 34). If Barak were a coward, why would he receive such commendation in Scripture?

Another conservative scholar, Thomas Schreiner of Bethel Theological Seminary, dismisses Deborah's authority by insisting that she "did not exercise a public ministry" like other prophets.[3] (Actually the Bible says in Judges 4:5 that she did her prophesying in public, under a palm tree in "the hill country.") Schreiner also contends that Deborah "did not exercise leadership over men as the other judges did."[4] (This is a laughable suggestion, since Judges 4:5 plainly says "the sons of Israel came to her for judgment.")

Conservative theologians love to typecast Barak as some kind of weak-kneed wimp who wanted a mother figure to go into battle with him. That was not Barak's problem. He had plenty of testosterone. He was a man's man—most likely a brave general. But he knew that Israel had no chance to win this war against the superior armies of the Canaanites unless God performed a military miracle. Barak did, in fact, expect that miracle, but he knew it would not happen unless God's appointed prophet went along. That is why he wanted Deborah by his side. It had nothing to do with her gender. He knew that only God's power could defeat a hostile army equipped with nine hundred iron chariots.

But what about Deborah's prophecy about a woman taking the top honor when the battle was finished? She was, of course, referring to the maiden Jael, who drove a tent peg into Sisera's skull after all the other Canaanite warriors had been slaughtered (Judg. 4:21). Did Jael's triumphant deed indicate that God was not pleased with Barak or that he should not have asked for Deborah to accompany him into battle?

The Bible never says that God was displeased with Barak. The fact that his name appears in Hebrews 11:32 as an example of courageous faith confirms this. In addition, Deborah's victory song in Judges 5 makes it clear that Barak's valor rallied Israel and helped win the war. Because he was humble enough to listen to God's prophet and to put his trust in the Lord, Israel conquered the Canaanites. And because he was willing to listen to God speak through a woman, Barak's humility released a woman to rise up and strike the final blow.

It is interesting that rabbis in later Jewish history cast Deborah in a negative light, even though the Bible praises her. They actually developed a play on her name, which means "bee," and changed it to "hornet." According to researchers Larry and Sue Richards, these rabbis "implied that [Deborah] was an arrogant woman who stung rather than provided good things for her people."[5]

This same antagonism against Deborah is evident today among some traditionally minded Bible scholars. They want us to believe that Deborah never should have judged Israel in the first place or that her story proves women should not hold senior positions of authority. But the Bible does not suggest such a ridiculous conclusion. God put Deborah in her place in the Old Testament to foreshadow the day when the Holy Spirit would anoint many prophetesses to stand as leaders in His church.

I've also heard conservative scholars make the outlandish claim that God allowed Deborah to serve as a judge in Israel because the nation was backslidden—as if female leadership is a type of spiritual curse. If this were the case, then why did Israel most often have wicked kings on the throne during periods of apostasy and spiritual waywardness? And if female leadership is a form of judgment, why did God bless Israel during Deborah's forty-year tenure as a national prophet? Such arguments are not rational.

If we learn the intended lesson of Deborah's story, the church today would experience more Jael-style victories. And if we had more men like Barak, who trusted the Lord and had the sense to listen when God was speaking through one of His female servants, the enemy's army would be fleeing rather than gaining ground. Deborahs and Jaels function in a New Testament setting, too, but they need some Baraks who are willing to support them.

Question #15
The Good Ol'
Boys' Club

If women can have leadership roles in the church, why didn't Jesus have female disciples?

I once was asked this question during a dinner with a group of bishops from the largest African American Pentecostal denomination in the United States. This group does not ordain women as pastors, and all of the twelve bishops in its presiding board are male. Like many churches in this country, women are barred from senior leadership positions because its leaders believe that God never intended women to serve "at the top."

When I asked one of the group's bishops why women could not serve as pastors, he shot back with an instant reply: "Because Jesus did not have women disciples. If Jesus didn't put women in leadership, then we shouldn't either."

That might sound like a rational biblical policy, but I learned that this denomination tiptoes on both sides of the issue. This group has a history of sending women pioneers to start new churches. Rather than calling the women "pastors," they refer to them as "shepherdesses"—as if this more obscure title denotes less authority. It's a sneaky way to get around the church's own rule.

These shepherdesses win new converts, organize prayer meetings, conduct outreaches and lead worship services until the congregation grows big enough to be considered a tithing church. At that point a man is sent to take over. So in the case of this denomination, women were allowed to do all the work of a pastor (in fact, they were sent to do the hardest part of a pastor's job!), but they were never allowed to carry the title or hold the position officially. They could only do it covertly, almost as if God did not notice that they were bending their religious traditions to get the job done.

Sometimes the way we handle the issue of women ministers is laughable. We make rigid rules to keep women out of leadership, but we can't run the church without their involvement. We don't want them at the top, but we need their money because they are usually the most faithful givers—and they often make up the majority of the congregation.

But we do need to examine this question in all seriousness: Does the fact that Jesus' disciples were all male set a precedent that women cannot serve in senior leadership?

How Would Jesus Feel About Women Disciples?

It is interesting that Jesus never once addressed this issue or issued any kind of rule about it. He never once said, "All leaders in My church must be men"—yet He went out of His way to confront the oppression of women in Israel. If we look closer at the Gospels, we will see three reasons why we can't use Jesus' male disciples as an excuse to deny women positions of authority.

1. *Jesus* did *have women on his team.*

Anyone who claims that Jesus did not have female disciples is not reading the Bible correctly. Luke 8:1–3 says that in addition to "the twelve," a group of women also followed Jesus. These women included Mary Magdalene, Joanna, Susanna and "many others who were contributing to their support out of their private means." These women were not just cooking breakfast for the guys or fetching water and food. They were in training.

We cannot overlook the fact that it was very unorthodox of Jesus to allow women to be a part of His entourage. Jewish rabbis in Jesus' day did not have female disciples; their oral tradition taught that it was shameful to even teach a woman from the Torah.[1] Talmudic tradition also specified that men should not be seen with women in public or talk to them. Yet Jesus welcomed women to study under His tutelage, and He did not hide His female followers from the watchful eyes of His religious critics.

It is very possible that the Pharisees were observing when Mary was bold enough to sit at Jesus' feet while He was teaching in her home. Sitting at the feet of a rabbi was a public statement; it meant that the person seated on the floor was a disciple. No woman in Israel had ever dared to take the posture of a disciple before because rabbis viewed women as ignorant, filthy, immoral and the source of all evil. But Mary knelt in front of her Teacher because Jesus made women feel comfortable in that position. When Martha begged her sister to return to the kitchen, Jesus affirmed Mary's place at His feet by saying, "Mary has chosen the good part, which shall not be taken away from her" (Luke 10:42).

Women knew that Jesus had a different spirit from all the other chauvinistic rabbis of the day. When the Pharisees were ready to execute a woman for adultery (even though their supposed "evidence" was questionable), Jesus was moved with compassion and came to her defense. When He healed the woman who had been bleeding for twelve years, He referred to her as "Daughter" (Luke 8:48), an endearing term that no rabbi would have used.

When Jesus carried on a theological discussion with the woman at the well in Samaria, she led her entire village to faith because she had never met a rabbi who demonstrated such love and acceptance (John 4). When He healed the woman in the temple whose back was bent over, he referred to her—in the presence of the Pharisees—as "a daughter of Abraham" (Luke 13:16). This surely caused a stir among His critics because "daughter of Abraham" was not a commonly used term among rabbis. They often referred to men as "sons of Abraham," but they denied women the blessings of the Abrahamic covenant.

Jesus most definitely had women followers, and they stayed close by His side until the end—even when the Twelve became cowards and hid from the authorities after the crucifixion. Some of the women stood near the Savior's cross, then they showed up on Easter morning to attend to His body in spite of the risk that Roman guards would arrest them. Their bravery made them the first witnesses of His Resurrection. How ridiculous that we would suggest that Jesus did not have women disciples, when it was these women who inaugurated the preaching of the gospel after He told them: "Go and take word to My brethren..." (Matt. 28:10).

2. The group known as "the Twelve" represented a symbolic new beginning.

Jesus often spoke in parables, and He frequently engaged in prophetic acts and used prophetic symbolism. Prophetic signs accompanied His birth; Magi from the East came to His crib with royal gifts to signify that the Gentile nations would one day worship Him as King. His baptism occurred at the Jordan River because it was on that site that Israel entered the Promised Land centuries before.

And there was a prophetic reason why Jesus chose twelve Jewish males to be His closest disciples. On one hand, they represented the twelve tribes of Israel, and Jesus used them to signify that He had come to call the lost Jewish nation to repentance and rebirth. The Twelve also were a quiet reminder of the spies who were sent out by Moses into the Promised Land; yet these men would be commissioned to conquer not just Canaan, but all the world.

But Jesus did not create this prophetic group to be exclusive or to make a statement about gender. After all, every man in the group known as *the Twelve* was a Jew. There was not one Gentile among them. Was this because Jesus intended for only Jewish males to serve as leaders in the church? Of course not. Immediately after the outpouring of the Holy Spirit on the Day of Pentecost, the newly empowered Christians took their message to Samaria, Asia Minor, Greece and eventually Rome. Within a few short years there were Gentile leaders in the church—including a Roman woman named Junia! (See Romans 16:7.)

Yes, it is true that the original twelve disciples were male. Just as Adam was created first, the men were the initiators. They were the "heads," or the point of origin. But just as Eve was taken from Adam's side, women disciples came alongside their male counterparts to fulfill a kingdom purpose. Though they did not come first, they were equally endowed with the Spirit's power and were granted equal access to the Spirit's giftings and callings. Nothing in Scripture denies them that place.

3. Jesus had a long-range plan for redemption.

I've heard people say, "If Jesus meant for women to serve in leadership positions, then He could have put at least one woman among the Twelve." That argument doesn't work, since Jesus was not in a hurry to dismantle every form of oppression in the world during His earthly ministry.

Jesus never directly confronted the institution of slavery, for example, yet the power of the gospel eventually ended the slave trade many hundreds of years later. He did not wage a campaign against racism in Israel, but when the message of the gospel took root in the Roman Empire, it demolished barriers of class and race. Jesus did not come to establish a form of government in Israel, but the gospel's influence ended the cruelty of Roman dictatorship after just three hundred years and planted the seeds of democracy, civil rights and the Christian rule of law that would one day become the norm.

In the same way, the message of the gospel contained the seeds that would one day release women from cultural oppression. The infant churches that sprung up in the first and second centuries in Turkey, Greece and Italy offered unprecedented opportunities for women to be trained in the Scriptures and to serve as elders, deacons, pastors, prophets, evangelists, teachers and even missionary apostles. This grand liberty for women is imbedded in the Christian message at its core.

To suggest that the Twelve somehow represent a barrier to women in ministry is to read chauvinism into the text. Jesus was not a chauvinist. After the advent of the Spirit, His first male disciples realized that the kingdom was not about exclusion but about community, liberty and love.

Question **#16**
Are Women Elders Called Elderettes?

My pastor told me that the list of qualifications for elders in the New Testament make it clear that only men can serve in that role. Can women be elders in a local church?

Y our pastor's position on women elders is typical in conservative Christian circles, but it is based more on cultural bias than on sound biblical interpretation. I believe that if we approach the Scriptures without preconceived religious mind-sets and depend on revelation from the Holy Spirit, we will find that the Bible frees women to assume leadership roles in the local church. The Scriptures also leave room for women to be appointed to every one of the five ministry offices mentioned in Ephesians 4:11—apostle, prophet, pastor, teacher and evangelist.

Women in Ministry With Paul

We know that the apostle Paul had women on his team and that he empowered them with authority. Let's examine a few of these leaders:

Priscilla (Acts 18:18–21; 24–28; Rom. 16:3)

Priscilla was a skilled teacher who had been trained by Paul himself. She and her husband, Aquila, traveled throughout the Roman world strengthening newly established churches. The Bible often mentions her name before Aquila's, most likely because she had a more visible teaching ministry. Some scholars believe that because she was Roman, she may have been from a wealthy family with access to education that most women did not have. Others have theorized that she may have written the Book of Hebrews, but this cannot be proven. A fascinating study of this theory appears in the book *Priscilla's Letter* by Ruth Hoppin (Lost Coast Press, 2000).

Phoebe (Rom. 16:1–2)

Paul describes Phoebe as a deacon. The passage says, "I commend to you our sister Phoebe, who is a *diakonos* of the church which is at Cenchrea" (v. 1). The word *diakonos* is always translated "minister" or "deacon" when applied to men, but the word is curiously translated in this verse as "servant" in many versions. Is this because Bible translators were uncomfortable with a woman holding a governmental office?

In Romans 16:2, Paul refers to Phoebe as a *prostatis*, which can be translated "presiding officer." The term definitely carries with it a significant weight of authority, so we can conclude that Phoebe was not simply running a women's ministry or setting up Sunday schools for children. She was an envoy of Paul's, carrying apostolic directives—and Paul expected the churches to listen to her. Catherine Kroeger points out that *prostatis* is often used in the writings of the early church fathers to denote someone who presided over communion.[1]

Junia (Rom. 16:7)

Up until the thirteenth century, no one questioned the name of this woman mentioned in Romans 16:7. Junia is a common Roman name. However, translators later began changing her name to "Junias" or "Junianus" because they could not accept the idea that Paul would refer to a woman as "outstanding among the apostles." But the original New Testament has it right, and we don't need to tamper with the language to fit our chauvinism. Paul singled out this woman because of her apostolic courage and for the fact that she suffered in prison alongside Paul. We don't have record of her ministry activities, but we can assume that she was probably involved in preaching and church planting.

Even early church father John Chrysostom (347–407), who was by no means sympathetic to women, acknowledged that Junia held a powerful position in the New Testament church. He wrote in his commentary on Romans: "Indeed, to be an apostle at all is a great thing; but to be even amongst those of note: just consider what a great encomium that is. Oh, how great is the devotion of this woman, that she should be even counted worthy of the appellation of Apostle." [2]

Nympha (Col. 4:15)

Paul asked the leaders of the Colossian church to "greet Nympha and the church that is in her house." Traditionalists would argue that this woman was simply "hosting" the church while men carried out the pastoral ministry, but that then begs the question: Why did Paul mention her rather than the male leaders? Was she just a hostess, making cookies and sandwiches for Paul and his team? Was Paul fond of Nympha because she served his favorite meals when he visited? It is more probable that she had been designated to lead the church that met in her home.

To suggest that Nympha was a pastor, of course, opens up a can of worms for traditionalists who believe the Bible limits this office to men. But does it? In Ephesians 4:11, when Paul explains that Jesus has given pastors, teachers, evangelists, apostles and prophets to the church for its edification, he makes no rules about gender. The "no women pastors" rule—so common in many denominations—is a religious tradition, not a biblical precept.

In the Book of Acts, we read about the woman Lydia (Acts 16:14–15, 40), an influential businesswoman who became the first European convert to Christianity. It is most likely that Lydia played a role in securing Paul's release from the Philippian magistrates since she had wealth and, most likely, political prestige. (The Acts account mentions in 16:40 that Paul returned to Lydia's house after he demanded a trial.) Some scholars suggest that Lydia's story was included in the Book of Acts because she eventually pastored a church in her home and became a crucial member of Paul's apostolic team as he pushed the gospel westward into the new continent.

Euodia and Syntyche (Phil. 4:2–3)

Paul considered these women "fellow workers ... who have shared my struggle" (v. 3). It is possible that they had been imprisoned with him for their preaching. Whatever the case, they were definitely not just female members of the church at Philippi. They were leaders, and they were having a serious disagreement—so serious that Paul had to urge them to "live in harmony in the Lord" (v. 2).

Paul does not say that either woman was teaching false doctrine. Perhaps their disagreement was over methodology, or perhaps they allowed jealousy or personal ambition to drive a wedge between them. We will never know what caused the tension between these two women, but we do know that Paul did not blame their division on gender. He didn't say, "Tell those women pastors that they don't have any business in the ministry. Women are too petty and emotional to be pastors." If Paul did not support women in such roles, he surely would not have commended them as ministry colleagues.

Women pastors emerge in other places in the New Testament. The apostle John's second epistle is addressed to "the chosen lady and her children" (2 John 1), and based on the letter's content, it is most certainly addressed to a church that was combating heresy. The "elect lady" is most likely the church's pastor or elder; I seriously doubt John would have used such feminine terminology if the pastor were a man. Yet conservative scholars dismiss this woman by saying that she was either the "hostess" of the church (providing safety or financial assistance) or that "elect lady" (KJV) is some kind of code word for a local congregation. Such an interpretation seems to ignore the obvious.

Besides these women who held offices in the fivefold ministry, the Bible also leaves room for women to hold positions of senior leadership or eldership in the local church. But Bible translators have not made it easy for us to defend their positions. In fact, blatant sexism has been applied in key passages that mention women leaders.

1 Timothy 3:1–13

In this passage Paul listed qualifications for men who aspire to the office of an overseer or church elder. He addressed these men first; then he listed qualifications for male deacons. Third, he addressed a category of women. Many translations of the Bible call these women "wives of deacons," but this is an erroneous translation. It should simply be translated "the women."

What women? The wives of church leaders? No, the word is not "wives." What Paul was addressing here is a category of women leaders who obviously had responsibility in the local congregation.

Like the men, they had to exhibit a higher standard of character. This is why he called them to be "dignified, not malicious gossips, but temperate, faithful in all things" (v. 11).

Titus 1:5–2:10

In this passage, Paul told Titus how to set up the government of a local church, and then he gave qualifications for "older men" and "older women." Was he talking about how senior citizens in the church should act? No—he was talking about *male elders* and *female elders*. How do we know this? The Greek word used for "older men" is *presbytas*, and the word for "older women" in this passage is *presbytidas*. A similar word, *presbytera*, is used in 1 Timothy 5:2. It means female elder, and it refers to an office in the church.[3]

Catherine Kroeger notes that these women (who had responsibility for teaching the women in the church, see verse 4) are urged in Titus 2:3 to act "worthy of sacred office."[4] (Some translations, like the New American Standard Bible, say, "Be reverent in their behavior.") In fact, one New Testament dictionary translates this adjective to say "like those employed in sacred service."[5] If Paul were simply addressing the behavior of older women in general, why would he expect them to "act like" they were in full-time ministry? He was addressing women in full-time ministry!

1 Timothy 5:1–8

Paul also mentioned another category of women leaders in the New Testament church known as "the widows." These were not just women whose husbands had died; they were an "order" of women who served in a full-time capacity much like deacons. Churches in Paul's day employed these women to serve in various capacities, most likely ministering to the sick, helping orphans, organizing outreach projects or carrying out pastoral duties. Whatever their specific role, they most definitely were empowered with authority to carry out the work of ministry. It is tragic that the modern church has not harnessed the energies and spiritual gifts of older women in this way.

The record of early church history proves that women were functioning in all these roles during the first centuries after Pentecost. Archeology also has proven it: Tombstones, coffins and other markers from the second and third century have provided numerous examples of women who were called *presbyteras*. We also know that women in these early centuries of the church served as missionaries and Bible teachers. One of them, St. Thelca, was known as an apostle, and the remains of a training center she founded have been excavated on a site near the ancient city of Seleucia.[6] Another powerful female leader, Pulcheria, helped overcome early heresies, and she defended the biblical doctrine of Christ's nature at the Council of Calcedon.[7]

There is ample evidence from the Bible and history that women served in these key leadership roles in the church. By forbidding them to serve, we quench the Holy Spirit in our sisters and deprive God's people of gifts and anointings that were intended to be shared freely. We would certainly see more spiritual victory if the Deborahs, Nymphas, Priscillas, Phoebes and Junias of our day were given equal opportunity.

Question #17
Shhh! Be Quiet, Girls!

My pastor told me that women should be silent in church. He was quoting the apostle Paul in 1 Corinthians 14:34–35. How should we view that verse of Scripture?

Many conservative evangelical Christians who take pride in the fact that they believe the Bible is inerrant, and who believe that every verse should be taken "literally," do not treat 1 Corinthians 14:34–35 that way. If they did, it would mean that women could never utter one word in a church service. Women could not say a prayer, make an announcement, sing a song or read the Bible aloud—much less preach a sermon!

Even in the most fundamentalist churches in the United States, where women are excluded from all leadership positions and never encouraged to pursue public ministry, women are permitted to sing in choirs, read from the Bible and pray publicly (although they are sometimes prohibited from doing this from the pulpit). Yet these same churches exclude women from the role of pastor or teacher on the basis of 1 Corinthians 14:34–35. It is a curious double standard, especially for those who claim to be such biblical literalists. After all, this passage does not simply limit women from pastoring or preaching—it completely muzzles them!

Let's look at the passage carefully:

> Let the women keep silent in the churches; for they are not permitted to speak, but let them subject themselves, just as the Law also says. And if they desire to learn anything, let them ask their own husbands at home; for it is improper for a woman to speak in church.

These are strong words. In fact, most English translations soften the blow, because the latter portion of verse 35 should actually read, "...the voice of a woman is obscene." How could Paul make such a seemingly crude and sexist statement? After all, in this same letter to the church at Corinth, in the eleventh chapter, he gave guidelines for women praying and prophesying in a church meeting (1 Cor. 11:5). Is this not a contradiction? Also, we know that Paul commissioned women, including Phoebe, Priscilla and Chloe, to positions of leadership and service. How could they fulfill these roles without speaking?

This passage triggers all kinds of questions. What law is this passage referring to when it says women must be silent "as the Law also says"? There is certainly no law in the Old Testament that forbids women from speaking. And why are the women asked to go home and talk to their husbands? Does this passage imply that women are stupid? It certainly sounds like the author is not giving the women of this church much credit.

Most traditionalists have come up with an easy answer by adopting what I call the "noisy women theory." It suggests that the Corinthian church faced a unique problem created by boisterous, uneducated women who were interrupting the church meeting in order to ask questions or make remarks about the lesson. Since it is assumed that women were seated in a special section of the room, they would have had to shout their questions in order to be heard. (Women in some Jewish synagogues were actually cloistered in an enclosed balcony so that they could not even be seen, much less heard.)

Some Bible scholars have theorized that the directive given in this passage, "Let the women keep silent," does not refer to all forms of speech, but rather to the kind of noisy, boisterous clamor created by these Corinthian women. After all, if the women who huddled together in the back of this church were uneducated, and if they were clueless about what was being said by the teacher, perhaps they started their own discussions among themselves. This chattering would certainly create a distraction. If they stood and asked a silly question or perhaps tried to inject an irrelevant comment, the teacher in charge might never be able to finish his sermon.

If this is the case, it makes 1 Corinthians 14:34–35 the equivalent of a "PLEASE KEEP QUIET" sign in a library. But can it be used to limit the ministries of trained, ordained female ministers?

While the noisy women theory sounds plausible (and is often published in commentaries and study notations in various versions of the Bible), there are several unresolved problems that remain:

1. We still haven't answered what "Law" (v. 34) restricts female speech. The Bible does not prohibit women from speaking, and we have several Old Testament examples of female prophets.

2. Why would Paul say, "If [the women] desire to learn anything, let them ask their own husbands at home"? The tone is condescending, as if he does not believe

that most women want to learn spiritual things. Yet we know from Paul's ministry that he ministered to female converts such as Lydia and discipled them.

3.   Why would Paul, who ordained Phoebe as a deacon and Junia as an apostle, say that it is "improper" for a woman to speak in church? The King James Version translates it this way: "It is a shame for women to speak in church." How can this be?

The mystery of 1 Corinthians 14:34–35 can be solved by using what I call the "inserted comment theory." It proposes that the statements in verses 34 and 35 were not written by Paul, but were taken from the letter that had been written to him by the leaders of the congregation in Corinth. Paul quoted them in his letter, and then replied to them beginning in verse 36.

How do we know this? The Greek language does not have quotation marks, but the symbol η (with a grave accent) is used after quoted material to denote that it was taken from another source. This symbol appears at the end of verse 35.[1]

In other places in 1 Corinthians, Paul quoted from a letter that had been sent by the leaders in Corinth. In 1 Corinthians 7:1, he tells them:

> Now concerning the things *about which you wrote,* it is good for a man not to touch a woman.
>
> —EMPHASIS ADDED

Paul acknowledges here that he is writing his epistle in response to a letter from the leaders of the Corinthian church, and he addresses each of their concerns one by one—from biblical sexuality, to women's head coverings, to a dispute about meat sacrificed to idols. In chapter 7, is it Paul who says, "It is good for a man not to touch a woman"? No! Paul did not believe that sex was evil. He refutes this idea in the next verse by stating clearly that sex is good and blessed by God when it remains within the confines of marriage.

Paul was quoting a slogan used by the Corinthians—a slogan that represented a serious heresy that forbade marriage and sex altogether. This "don't touch women" heresy spread throughout the early church in the second and third centuries; it deceived Christians into believing that men should abstain from sex and live in monasteries while women retreated to convents.

Just as Paul quoted the Corinthian leaders' letter in 1 Corinthians 7:1, he did the same thing with verses 34 and 35 in chapter 14. This explains why Paul said, "What?" in his response in verse 36.

Let's examine this passage in the King James Version:

> What? came the word of God out from you? or came it unto you only? If any man think himself to be a prophet, or spiritual, let him acknowledge that the things that I write unto you are the commandments of the Lord. But if any man be ignorant, let him be ignorant.
>
> —1 Corinthians 14:36–38

In modern language, Paul is saying, "Huh?" He was probably shaking his head in bewilderment when these leaders told him that they did not allow women to speak in church. He asks in verse 36, "Was it from you that the word of God first went forth?" He is chiding them for their arrogance here, reminding them that the first people to announce the gospel on Easter morning were the women disciples who had followed Jesus faithfully. If Jesus chose women to be the first witnesses of His Resurrection, why would we forbid them to teach, testify, sing, prophesy or pray in church?

Paul dismissed their argument abruptly, and then said, "If any man be ignorant, let him be ignorant." This was more than a mild rebuke. He confronted their sexist views of women with stinging sarcasm—by inferring that it was the men in this situation who were acting stupidly, not the women.

If verses 34 and 35 were indeed authored by the leaders at Corinth, and not Paul, then this helps us understand what "Law" they were referring to. The church at Corinth was guided by men who had a Jewish background. In fact, most leaders in the Christian church in the early period were converted Jews. This created a serious problem with legalism, because the Jews who embraced the gospel still wanted to impose their many traditions on Gentile converts. Paul spent a vast amount of his time helping Jewish Christians understand that a new covenant of grace, made possible by the indwelling Holy Spirit, had superceded the requirements of legalistic, performance-based religion.

Jewish rabbis based their faith not simply on the Old Testament but on a huge volume of laws and commentaries compiled by rabbis. This collection of sayings, preserved orally and memorized by rabbis and their disciples, came to be known as the Mishnah, which was first recorded in writing sometime around A.D. 200. A later volume of rabbinical commentaries on the Mishnah came to be known as the Talmud.[2] The laws included in the Mishnah went much further than Old Testament laws, adding detailed conditions and requirements for human behavior, including elaborate rules about Sabbath-keeping, diet and sexual practice.

The Mishnah and other rabbinical codes had plenty to say about women—and none of it was positive. Three ancient versions of the Mishnah contain a prayer that says: "Praise be to God he has not created me a Gentile; praise be to God that he has not created me a woman; praise be to God that he has not created an ignorant man."[3] Rabbinical writings contained many other degrading comments and baffling laws about women, including these:

- A woman is not allowed to light the Sabbath lamp because she deceived Adam and "was the cause of his death."

- A woman's menstrual cycle represents the curse of God on women.

- The birth of a boy brings joy, but the birth of a girl brings sadness.

- All women are by nature greedy, eavesdroppers, slothful and envious.

- Men who talk with women bring evil upon themselves and will end up in hell.

- Serious students of the Torah should abstain from sex with their wives for as long as three years.

- Children are born "dead" because they originated from a woman's womb and had to look at it at birth.

- Women in the synagogue had to be seated at least fifteen steps away from the men.

- A woman must always cover her head because she is the object of shame.

- If a wife does not accept her husband's control, he should divorce her.[4]

Charles Trombley points out that divorce laws in rabbinical writings were beyond ridiculous:

> If a woman ate in the street, drank greedily in the
> street, or suckled her baby in the street, she could be
> divorced. If she gossiped, spun in the moonlight, left
> her hair unfastened, spun in the street with her
> armpits uncovered, or bathed in the same place as
> men, she could be divorced. If she was childless for a
> ten-year period, her husband could put her away.[5]

These legalistic rules—which have no basis whatsoever on biblical truth—guided ancient Judaism and were the primary focus of
the Pharisees in Jesus' day. He often rebuked them for placing more
importance on their man-made codes of law than on God's Word.
In one instance, when the Pharisees questioned Jesus about why His
disciples did not wash their hands according to rabbinical rules, He
asked them, "Why do you yourselves transgress the commandment
of God for the sake of your tradition?" (Matt. 15:3).

Jesus often told the Pharisees that their religious formulas were
offensive to God. In a heated exchange with the leaders of the
Pharisees, Jesus even quoted their rabbinical code when He cor-
rected them. In Matthew 15:4–6, Jesus quoted one of their rabbinical laws that made it possible for people to excuse themselves
from caring for elderly parents:

> For God said, "Honor your father and mother," and,
> "He who speaks evil of father or mother, let him be
> put to death." But you say, "Whoever shall say to his
> father or mother, 'Anything of mine you might have
> been helped by has been given to God,' he is not to
> honor his father or his mother." And thus you invali-
> dated the word of God for the sake of your tradition.

Just as Jesus quoted the Mishnah in this passage, Paul quoted
the chauvinistic oral tradition that had been instituted as religious

practice in the New Testament church at Corinth. The apostle did not endorse their chauvinism, nor did he approve of the silencing of women. Paul would never have allowed such spiritual bondage, and neither should we. Modern Pharisees will continue to make their religious rules to silence or hinder women—but we should respond with the apostle's astonishment and say to them: "What?" Oppression of women has no place in the church of God. Where the Spirit is, there is liberty.

Question #18
It's All About Eve

My pastor does not allow women to teach or preach in a worship service. He says that because Eve was deceived in the Garden of Eden, women naturally lead people into deception. Does the Bible really say this?

Back in the 1980s, a prominent female author and evangelist was invited to address a conference sponsored by her conservative denomination. When it came time for her to speak, she approached the podium and opened her Bible. Then, a loud commotion began toward the front of the auditorium. She looked down to see several rows of men, all in their dark suits, quickly turning their chairs around. Within a few moments, it was obvious what was happening. These men, all pastors, had turned their backs to this woman to protest her inclusion in the program. They were making a statement. In their narrow theological view, it is wrong for women to teach the Bible to men. So in a rather flamboyant way, they refused to listen to her message—lest the sound of her words pull them away from true faith just as the mythological sirens lured Greek sailors to their deaths.

I heard this woman teach at a large church in Orlando, Florida, a few years later during a clergy conference sponsored by Campus Crusade for Christ. Her name is Anne Graham Lotz, and she is one of evangelist Billy Graham's three daughters. There was no false doctrine or faulty teaching in anything she said.

The night Anne spoke at Orlando's First Baptist Church, the auditorium was packed, mostly with male ministers and a few ministers' wives. Her sermon was engaging, her North Carolina drawl made me feel welcome, and her preaching style and cadence seemed eerily similar to her father's, even though she delivered it in a completely feminine manner. She called the audience to pursue a real relationship with God rather than a religious lifestyle. And when the meeting was over that evening, most people would have agreed that Anne had preached better than any of the men who had stood at the podium that week.

Thankfully, no one in the Orlando conference attempted to turn a chair around to protest this gifted woman's message. But many women who have legitimate ministry calls today are still being given the cold shoulder and are treated with shocking disrespect. It is usually because of what we could call "the Eve factor."

The faulty logic goes like this: Eve was deceived by the devil; therefore, all women are capable of being deceived and, in turn, of deceiving others. In order to protect the church from deception, we must keep all the daughters of Eve out of the pulpit, or so the notion says. Fortunately for men, the same logic has not been applied to males. After all, Adam rebelled against God by partaking of the forbidden fruit, yet we do not seem to be concerned that every man who stands in the pulpit will automatically lead the church into rebellion simply because he is a "son of Adam."

This idea that women are to blame for all of society's ills is not a biblical notion, but it became part of Christian tradition because of the writings of the early church fathers in the second, third and fourth centuries. Tertullian (160–225) called women "the devil's gateway"—and he stated in no uncertain terms that woman must forever bear Eve's guilt.[1] Origen (185–254) had no use for any teaching from a woman. He once wrote: "It is not proper for a woman to speak in church, however admirable or holy what she says may be, merely because it comes from female lips."[2]

Another revered church father, Ambrose (340–397), taught unashamedly that men are superior to women. "Woman is inferior to man, she is part of him, she is under his command. Sin began with her, she must wear this sign, the veil."[3] Indeed, many of the early patriarchs of the church taught that women, especially virgins, should always cover themselves with full veils. They also taught that a man's beard, his body hair and his genitals were nature's proof of masculine superiority. Clement of Alexandria (150–215) said that a man's beard was a "badge" that "shows him unmistakably to be a man." The beard, he added, "is older than Eve and is a symbol of the stronger nature."[4]

Augustine (354–430), who influenced so many of the Protestant reformers, held many degrading views about women and lived them out by keeping a mistress. He taught that women are not even created in God's image, and he believed that women represented "the flesh" while men embodied "the spirit." He also adopted the chauvinistic views of ancient Jewish rabbis when he wrote, "Woman stands under the lordship of man and possesses no authority; she can neither teach, or be a witness."[5]

Scripture contradicts these degrading views of women. So did Jesus when He extended kindness, compassion and redemptive justice to so many women in His ministry. But the beliefs of the church fathers eventually became the prevalent philosophy in the medieval church, and they were adopted as well by Reformers, including Martin Luther and John Calvin. We are still haunted today by this phantom of male pride—which loves to disguise itself in religious garb.

It is indeed odd that we would use Eve to blacklist all women from teaching truth, especially since the Bible gives us so many examples of women who pointed the way to righteousness. One of those women was Huldah, a prophetess during the reign of King Josiah. Her story, recounted in 2 Kings 22, seems to fly in the face of the idea that women are "gateways of evil." In her case, Huldah was God's gateway to righteousness.

As the story goes, the king's emissaries discovered a neglected copy of the Book of the Law when they visited the abandoned temple (which was now a place to store implements used in the worship of Baal and Asherah). No one had been reading the scrolls of Moses in those days because Israel had become a backslidden nation. Not even King Josiah had been reading it. Israel had lost its way, and the very compass that could help the nation return to God had been buried under dust and cobwebs. When Josiah's secretary returned with the news of the lost scrolls, the king asked that they be read aloud.

When Josiah heard the words of Moses—which spoke of God's judgments on Israel if she forgot the Lord—he tore his robes and asked his staff to "go, inquire of the LORD for me" (v. 13). Josiah was sincerely repentant. Hearing the Word of God had smitten his conscience, and he desperately wanted to return to the Lord. But he also had sense enough to know he still had time. He wanted to know how he might still fit into God's plan. Whom would he ask? Who could point the way? Obviously, if the Book of the Law had been discarded in a forgotten chamber of the Lord's temple, there were very few people who would know what to do.

When Josiah's royal agents went looking for a word from God, the priest, Hilkiah, directed them to Huldah. Fortunately, this

priest was wise enough to know that God can speak ᴵ
woman. The Bible says Huldah lived in the second d.
Jerusalem (v. 14). We don't know anything about her, exc
her husband was the keeper of the priestly wardrobe. S
probably not a wealthy woman. God's prophets often te
emerge from obscurity and then disappear just as fast.

Whoever Huldah was, she knew God. And while the rest oᵣ
nation had been turning to idols, she had kept herself pure. ᵢ
was not a stranger to the forgotten book. Her prophecy, record
in 2 Kings 22:15–20, sounds just as authoritative as anythin
Jeremiah or Isaiah would have said:

> Because they have forsaken Me and have burned
> incense to other gods that they might provoke Me to
> anger with all the work of their hands, therefore My
> wrath burns against this place, and it shall not be
> quenched.
>
> —2 Kɪɴɢs 22:17

Huldah also gave a personal word of prophetic direction to
King Josiah, telling him that he himself would be spared injury
because of his repentant response. As a result of Huldah's directive,
Josiah undertook a sweeping program of ambitious reforms, in
which he purged the temple of Baal worship, tore down demonic
altars, rid the land of occultic practices, stopped child sacrifice,
executed priests who had led the people astray and reinstated the
celebration of Passover.

All this occurred because a woman pointed God's people in the
right direction. Huldah, unlike Eve, was not listening to the serpent.
Her ear was tuned to God at a time when no one else's was. Why,
then, are we not more open to giving the Huldahs of our day a place
of godly influence? I hope we don't wait until we face a national
emergency before we ask them to prophesy.

The Apostle Paul and Women

It is clear from Huldah's example that God can use women to teach and prophesy in an authoritative manner. But what do we do with the apostle Paul's words in 1 Timothy 2:12–14? This is the passage that is so often used to restrict women's ministry, and because Paul himself made a reference to Eve as being deceived, it has been used to bolster the argument that women will lead the church astray if they are given the opportunity. The passage reads this way in the King James Version:

> But I suffer not a woman to teach, nor to usurp authority over the man, but to be in silence. For Adam was first formed, then Eve. And Adam was not deceived, but the woman being deceived was in the transgression.
>
> —1 TIMOTHY 2:12–14, KJV

This is a curious passage indeed, and one that has puzzled Bible scholars for centuries. It is confusing for several reasons:

1. It seems to contradict how women have been used to speak for God in the Old Testament (women such as Deborah and Huldah, for example).

2. It does not fit Paul's own practice, since he had women teachers on his ministry team such as Priscilla, and he also encouraged women to be teachers (Titus 2:3–4).

3. Paul encourages women to prophesy in the local church meeting in 1 Corinthians 11:5 and invites equal participation in the exercising of spiritual gifts in the assembly (1 Cor. 12:7–11).

So what is Paul saying here?

If we take the passage at literal face value, we would have to say that women can never teach anyone, even small children. Conservative scholars bypass this interpretation by insisting that what Paul is restricting here is any form of "authoritative speech" that comes from women. If that is the case, would this not rule out Huldah's prophecy to King Josiah? Certainly we could describe her word of impending judgment, which was quickly ful-filled, as being authoritative. And what about the words of Deborah, which are included in the canon of Scripture in Judges 4 and 5? Are these not authoritative words, since they now carry the authority of holy Scripture? Would not Hannah's prayer in 1 Samuel 2:1–10, or Mary's exaltation in Luke 1:46–55, known as the *Magnificat*, also be considered authoritative speech?

Traditionalists who believe that Paul never allowed women to teach men in any setting or to hold positions of authority in the church must play games with these other portions of Scripture. That is why you rarely will hear a traditionalist preach on Deborah or Huldah.

But what do we do with Paul's words? There are two possible interpretations.

1. The women in Ephesus needed more instruction.

We should take note that this passage is preceded by another curious admonition from Paul to the women: "Let a woman qui-etly receive instruction with entire submissiveness" (1 Tim. 2:11). That might sound sexist to us today, but we must remember that women in this culture had been denied all educational opportu-nities. Except for some Roman women in the upper class, women in the Middle East and Asia Minor were sequestered at home and kept away from books and learning. The only thing men wanted them to learn was how to cook, fetch water, tend to the goats, keep house and raise the children.

Jewish rabbis, in fact, believed that it was even blasphemous to teach a woman the Torah. Jesus contradicted this view when He invited women to sit at His feet and learn. Paul, likewise, invited women to learn from God's Word—as long as they did it in a proper way—not like know-it-alls, but with a teachable spirit.

It is possible that the newly converted women in Ephesus were jumping the gun and trying to teach the gospel when they were not yet qualified. If this were the case, their ignorance would have created serious problems in the church. Paul would have had to put his foot down and say, "Enough is enough. Women aren't allowed to teach until they know what they are talking about."

But why would Paul mention a prohibition about teaching men? He could have been referring to the male teachers who were learned enough in theology to earn a platform in the Ephesian church. If women were standing up in the church meeting, asking questions or stating their own misguided views, or contradicting the elders, this would have created chaos in the church and usurped the authority of appointed leaders who were trained in doctrine.

And why would Paul have mentioned Adam and Eve? Gilbert Bilezikian suggests that Paul interjects the Garden of Eden story to remind the uneducated women of Ephesus that they have a lot to learn from those who have been instructed. He writes:

> In the fateful story of the fall, it was Eve, the lesser-informed person, who initiated a mistaken course of action and who led herself into error. Eve was not created first or at the same time as Adam. She was the late-comer on the scene. Of the two, she was the one bereft of the firsthand experience of God's giving the prohibition relative to the tree. She should have

deferred the matter to Adam, who was better prepared to deal with it since he had received the command directly from God. Regarding God's word, Adam had been teacher to Eve, and Eve the learner. Yet when the crisis arrived, she acted as the teacher and fell into the devil's trap. Her mistake was to exercise an authoritative function for which she was not prepared.[6]

If this is why Paul mentions Eve in his message to the Ephesians, one must ask: Was he laying down a permanent rule for all time that forbids women from teaching and exercising authority? Or was he issuing a correction that applied only to the situation in Ephesus? Knowing that Paul released other women like Priscilla to teach the Bible, and knowing that he set in place both men and women to function as leaders of the local church (1 Tim. 3:1–11), we must conclude that his words here were to correct the situation at hand.

After all, if Paul called the women to learn "in all submissiveness" to the Word of God, then surely he expected them to become mature disciples who would have the ability to teach others after receiving sufficient training.

2. The church in Ephesus was plagued by false teachers, some of them female.

Other scholars propose that Ephesus, a seat of paganism in the ancient world, was overrun by heresy and false doctrine because of various cults and Gnostic sects. Archeology does indicate that the cult of Diana, a mystic religion dominated by female priests, flourished in Ephesus at the time Timothy was leading the church there.

In the midst of this dilemma, one theory suggests, false teachers were infiltrating the infant church in Ephesus and leading people astray with their myths, false visions and fables. Richard and Catherine Clark-Kroeger, in their excellent book

I Suffer Not a Woman, propose that false teachers representing the Diana cult had crept into the church and were usurping authority from the teachers Paul had appointed.

One of the Gnostic fables that was commonly told at the time involved Eve. The Gnostics, who loved to turn a Bible story "upside down" in order to twist biblical truth, concocted the notion that Eve was created before Adam and that she actually liberated the world by listening to the serpent. In the pagan temples of the region around Ephesus, images of female deities are often depicted with serpent images.[7]

It is possible that one or more female false teachers had invaded the church at Ephesus and were spreading this detestable doctrine among the new Christians. Loren Cunningham, in his book *Why Not Women?*, suggests that Paul was actually singling out one female false teacher and that 1 Timothy 2:12 should be translated: "I do not allow *the woman* to teach or usurp authority."[8]

If this were indeed the scenario, Paul's words about Eve take on a different meaning. He may have been setting the record straight about Eve's creation order because this female false teacher had told the Ephesians two huge lies: (1) that Eve had been created first, and (2) that Eve had not been deceived by the serpent, but enlightened by him.

Paul then cleared up the confusion. "For Adam was formed first, then Eve. And Adam was not the one deceived; it was the woman who was deceived and became a sinner" (1 Tim. 2:13–14, NIV).

Whether Paul was fighting a false teacher in this case, or simply requiring women to receive proper instruction, we cannot use 1 Timothy 2:12 as a blanket prohibition against releasing women into ministry. Rather, this passage opens the door for women to be trained for public ministry and challenges them to handle the Word of God with accuracy. Obviously we do not need women ministers today who are undisciplined or untrained, or who are seeking to spread heresy. But we should by all means commission and ordain as many capable and anointed women as possible to advance the spread of the gospel. What we need in this crucial hour are women like Huldah who have studied God's Word and have the anointing to proclaim His counsel.

Question #19
Covered...
or Covered Up?

My church allows women to minister, but they say that a man must provide a spiritual "covering" for our prayer meetings or Bible studies. Is this a biblical policy?

The rule you are describing is quite common in many conservative evangelical churches, even though it is almost always an unwritten policy. I received a letter once from a woman who led a weekly women's Bible study. She told me that when the pastor learned that she planned to serve communion during the meeting, he told her that she could not do this unless a deacon or elder from the church was present. The elder did not have to serve the elements, but he had to be in the room to watch the proceedings.

Another woman I know who was organizing a women's conference was told that a man must be seated on the stage—even if he did not teach or say anything from the pulpit. In some denominations that sponsor women's conferences, a man is often appointed to fill at least one speaker's slot so that there can be a "male covering" for the event.

Is this a biblical policy? It is certainly acceptable to have a man speak at a women's conference. But there is no verse in Scripture that requires him to be there. The apostle Paul did not mention such a thing in his discussion of church order and spiritual gifts in 1 Corinthians 11 and 12—where he gives both men and women freedom to prophesy as the Holy Spirit directs. The leaders of the congregation in Corinth were arguing about whether a woman could pray or prophesy without wearing a veil or head covering—a cultural issue that we are not concerned about today.

When Paul instructed Titus that the older women (who were women elders, or presbyters) should "teach the young women," he did not add the condition that men should be present during the teaching (Titus 2:4, KJV). Obviously there were women's meetings occurring in the first-century church, and we can assume that they did not always have male supervision since this is never mentioned. The Bible does not say whether the women leaders were serving communion or baptizing new converts, but it is certainly feasible to believe that they were—especially since we know that other women, such as Paul's associate, Nympha, had been placed in charge of at least one congregation (Col. 4:15).

If the "male covering" policy is not a biblical rule, then where did this notion come from? We might find at least part of the answer by studying the history of the foreign missions movement.

It was not until the mid-1800s that a large number of women began to become involved in fulfilling the Great Commission. Until that time, except for a few shining beacons who were willing to challenge the status quo, most women assumed that only men could be evangelists or Bible teachers. But as the Holy Spirit's call went out concerning the desperate spiritual and physical needs in Africa and Asia, women began to respond—and men did not exactly know how to handle this dilemma.

Ruth Tucker and Walter Liefeld, in their book *Daughters of the*

Church, tell us that so many women responded to the call of world missions in the late 1800s that by 1894 there were thirty-three women's foreign mission boards. More than one thousand women were engaged in teaching, medical work or evangelism in foreign countries. One of the bold champions of this movement was Helen Barrett Montgomery, who wrote many books and comprehensive studies of female missionary achievements. In her book *Western Women in Eastern Lands,* she reported that between the years 1860 and 1910, this corps of unmarried women missionaries grew from 1 to 4,710, while women's missionary societies grew from 1 to 44.[1]

But Tucker and Liefeld point out that these newly appointed women missionaries caused no small stir on the field. In fact, many of them found disappointment once they arrived at their assignments because they were told they would not be allowed to do much more than teach girls' classes or serve as secretaries. Some, like Southern Baptist pioneer Lottie Moon, protested loudly; others were given liberty to teach or even start churches without interference. A few, like Mary Slessor, whose work in Calabar (now eastern Nigeria) paved the way for unprecedented revival there, convinced her superiors that a woman was more suited to reach hostile tribal chieftains because she would not intimidate them.[2]

But the Mary Slessors of the late 1800s rocked the boat too much, and there was a predictable reaction from traditionally minded men. Says Tucker and Liefeld: "The flocking of women into the field in the 1880s and 1890s led some general board officials to feel the need to remind women of their place."[3] One Baptist leader felt obligated to release this statement in 1888 to all workers on the field:

> Women's work in the foreign field must be careful to recognize the leadership of man in ordering the affairs of the kingdom of God. We must not allow the

major vote of the better sex, nor the ability and effi-
ciency of so many of our female helpers, nor even the
exceptional faculty for leadership and organization,
which some of them have displayed in their work, to
discredit the natural and predestined headship of
man in Missions, as well as in the Church of God: and
the "head of woman is man."[4]

Obviously, this Baptist leader did not believe in the equality of
men and women, even though he flatters them with his "better
sex" comment. We can forgive him for his patronizing attitude,
since he lived in a time period before women could even vote. It is
harder to understand why men today would still be unwilling or
unable to recognize that God can use women in extraordinary
ways, even when they are not being watched, or *covered*, by men.

The whole idea of requiring a male covering presents a myriad
of ridiculous questions. Does a woman need a man to cover her
when she shares her faith during a casual conversation on the
street? What if she feels called to evangelize female athletes? Must
she take a man with her into the locker room? What spiritual activities is a woman allowed to do without a man present? If she
cannot teach from a pulpit without a man sitting nearby, can she
write a book containing the same message—knowing that women
will read it without men watching? The argument becomes silly.

Biblical Principles for Women's Ministry

If you have been faced with this issue in your own church, I would
advise you not to trigger an argument with your pastor by
insisting that you don't need his or some other man's spiritual
covering. But you could graciously invite him to consider these
biblical principles as he develops a policy concerning women and
ministry:

25 TOUGH QUESTIONS ...

1. Headship pertains to marriage.

When church leaders raise the issue of male headship, they are referring to two passages in the New Testament: Ephesians 5:23 ("For the husband is the head of the wife"), and 1 Corinthians 11:3 ("the man is the head of a woman"). Some people have assumed that this means men have been designed by God to be the leaders in society, while women are called to be followers. And they assume this is God's model for the church as well.

But we need to be careful here, noting that in both of these passages Paul is discussing a wife's relationship with her husband, not a woman's relationship with all other men. In actuality, it would be a heretical concept to teach that all women are somehow to be placed in subjection to all men. Paul is not talking here about men and women in general. He is discussing marriage in particular.

If we investigate these two passages deeper, we discover that the concept of headship is not really about authority at all. It is about intimacy, mutuality and the unique connection that exists between a husband and wife. The word used here for "head" in the Greek is *kephale*, which can be translated "source," as the headwaters of a river are the source of the river. If Paul had meant to say, "The husband is the boss of the wife," or "The husband is the leader of the wife," he would have used the Greek word *archon*, which is often used in the New Testament to denote authority. (See the earlier discussion of these terms in chapter two.) He uses *kephale*, a rarer term.

Why would Paul say that the husband is the *source* of the wife? In both passages, he is referring to the origin of woman in the Garden of Eden. Adam was the "head," or "source," of Eve because she was taken from his side. And because she came from him, she as the wife enjoys a unique connection to him that cannot be paralleled by any other human relationship.

The headship principle, therefore, really has nothing to do with authority in the home. It stresses, rather, the *mutual dependence* that a man and wife have on each other, and it calls on husbands to nourish and cherish their wives since they have such an intimate connection with them in a spiritual sense. Theologian Gilbert Bilezikian says it best in his book *Beyond Sex Roles*:

> Because man as the fountainhead of woman's existence was originally used to supply her with her very life, and because he continues to love her sacrificially as his own body in marriage, in return a Christian wife binds herself to her husband in a similar relationship of servant submission that expresses their oneness. The imposition of an authority structure upon this exquisite balance of reciprocity would paganize the marriage relationship.[5]

Indeed, if male headship in marriage is not about top-down authority, then why would we impose such a hierarchical concept on male/female relationships in the church?

2. Spiritual authority is necessary.

While it is unbiblical to state that a woman must have a male covering to perform any kind of legitimate ministry, this does not mean she does not need to recognize spiritual authority. No woman who is called to ministry—and no man, for that matter— should be a spiritual Lone Ranger. Because we all have human frailties and are susceptible to the temptations of pride, deception and offense, we all need to be in fellowship with other mature believers who can provide guidance and correction as well as encouragement and counsel. That is why we have denominations, church networks and missionary agencies.

While I aggressively challenge women to enter the ministry, I would never counsel them to go it alone or to harbor a spirit of rebellion or independence. Women do not need a male covering to legitimize them, but they do in fact need a submissive attitude (and the same applies to men). God places authority in our lives to provide accountability, support and godly guidance. Whether that authority happens to be male or female is beside the point. God has placed both spiritual fathers and spiritual mothers in His family. But we are foolish if we think we can do it without them.

On the flip side, we also need to recognize that spiritual authority in the church, as revealed in the New Testament, is not about ecclesiastical control. We all know that men (and women) can organize a denominational structure with bishops, regional elders, policies, laws, programs and multi-level bureaucracy—and yet it can be completely devoid of the Holy Spirit's power. We gain nothing from submitting to such a structure.

The spiritual authority established in the Scriptures is the five-fold ministry of apostles, prophets, pastors, teachers and evangelists mentioned in Ephesians 4:11. And we are told that these gifted individuals are not to rule the church in a Gentile fashion, but rather "for the equipping of the saints for the work of service" (v. 12). They are releasing people into the liberty of Spirit-empowered ministry, not controlling the Holy Spirit in the lives of believers.

3. The anointing of the Holy Spirit is not restricted by gender.

It should be noted that women in the Bible—in both the Old and New Testaments—carried out ministry assignments and held positions of authority without the presence of men. The apostle Paul himself wrote to the church in Rome and asked them to support the woman named Phoebe, a deacon who served on Paul's apostolic team (Rom. 16:1–2).

Obviously Paul was not with Phoebe when she arrived from Cenchrea, since he was writing to the Romans from prison. But she was carrying out the work of the gospel, probably evangelizing and helping to organize new congregations, and Paul asked his colleagues to "receive her." He made no mention of any man traveling with her to act as her covering, and the Bible does not tell us whether she was single, married or widowed. Paul's endorsement of her was covering enough.

In the revival atmosphere of the early church, the Holy Spirit was moving too fast for the apostles to worry about whether women were posing a threat to their control. Paul and his apostolic colleagues were thrilled to have trained women on their teams, whether it was a deacon like Phoebe, an anointed Bible teacher like Priscilla or a woman like Junia, who was "outstanding among the apostles" (Rom. 16:7). I pray that the modern church will soon be allowed to enjoy the same atmosphere of liberty, and that we will reap the same supernatural results as the first-century apostles did.

Question **#20**
When Women
Are in Charge

I think it is wrong for a man to receive spiritual instruction or mentoring from a woman. Doesn't it emasculate a man if he submits to a woman in this way?

This is a common argument used by those who oppose women in church leadership. Some traditionalists contend that it is "against nature" for a woman to teach, lead or influence a man in a spiritual way. They believe that if a woman holds a position of authority over a man, he will lose his manhood by forfeiting his ability to lead. They also imply that by allowing women to hold leadership roles, the church will eventually lose all gender distinctions. ("After all," they ask, "if men and women can both lead, then what's the difference between the genders?") Others go so far as to suggest that placing women in roles of authority will unravel the fabric of family life and even encourage homosexuality.

In their book *Recovering Biblical Manhood and Womanhood*, evangelical scholars Wayne Grudem and John Piper make the case for what is known as the "complementarian" view of gender relationships. They contend, and rightly so, that the biblical family is under attack by secular humanists and feminists who want to rid the world of all gender distinctions. This is certainly a crisis that the church must address. Grudem and Piper's solution to this crisis, however, is that men should always be the leaders in the home and church, and that women should never assume the "role" of a leader in any capacity in church life—except in women's or children's ministry.

I would certainly agree that Christians must do everything possible to instill godly masculinity in our men and godly femininity in women. God never intended for the genders to be morphed or neutered. He is glorified by gender differences, and His divine nature is revealed through men and women in their unique characteristics (Gen. 1:27). Homosexuality is a crime against the nature of God because He chose to reveal Himself through male and female, and He instituted heterosexual marriage both for our enjoyment and for procreation.

God never intended for women to act masculine or for men to act feminine. He wants young boys to be affirmed in their masculinity by their fathers; likewise, mothers (as well as fathers) play a key role in affirming their daughters' femininity. But traditionalists err when they suggest that a man's masculinity is threatened when a woman assumes a leadership role, either as a teacher of the Bible or a spiritual overseer of some sort. The Scriptures do not uphold such a principle. Women can teach and lead in a feminine way that glorifies God. (And men who are threatened by female leadership may actually be suffering from a deep insecurity in their own masculinity.)

Let's use some logic here. If we are to believe that women exert a bad influence when they teach males, then why would we allow women to instruct boys in Sunday school, kindergarten or elementary school? The last time I checked, most teachers in our schools were female, and most churches leave children's ministry to the women since they've been excluded from leadership roles anyway. Isn't this a double standard? If we really believe boys are being damaged by all this feminine influence, why don't we insist that all male children must be taught by men?

Do female teachers in high schools emasculate teenage male pupils if they exercise authority over them? Should women teach men in college? Once men enter the work force, are they emasculated if they have female supervisors? The line of questioning becomes ridiculous.

And what about the impact of wise mothers on their sons? The Bible actually praises this motherly influence. In the Book of Proverbs, Solomon wrote, "Hear, my son, your father's instruction, *and do not forsake your mother's teaching*" (Prov. 1:8, emphasis added). If female authority figures are "against nature," why are there so many of them in Scripture? God's wisdom, in fact, is personified as a woman giving instruction, and her message is directed to men (Prov. 8:4).

Most Christian men I know who have made significant spiritual impact can list several "spiritual mothers" who influenced their growth and maturity in Christ. The influence of these women did not turn these men into sissies, nor did it lower their testosterone levels.

In December 2001 I interviewed one of the most prominent pastors in Nigeria, Bishop David Oyedepo. His congregation outside Lagos has the distinction of being housed in the world's largest church building. The main sanctuary, with fifty thousand seats, was filled to capacity on the Wednesday evening that I attended there. Another twenty thousand people were sitting or standing outside the building watching the service on a giant video screen.

Oyedopo, who is quite a visionary, has constructed a Christian university on his property—which he paid for with cash that he raised without any help from the United States. His ambitious goal is to train godly leaders who will someday transform Nigeria's dysfunctional social system.

When I asked this faith-filled man to tell me his testimony, he immediately smiled and expressed his gratitude for the missionaries who came to Nigeria from the West. A white woman who worked with the Scripture Union organization led him to Christ, he explained. She did not live to see how her young convert would transform Nigeria.

In January 2003 I met a fascinating missionary, Bahjet Batarseh, who has preached the gospel for fifty years and visited most countries in the world. Raised in Jordan, he has been used by God to reach millions of Muslims in nations like Pakistan, Egypt and Saudi Arabia. He estimates that more than one million people have been converted to Christ though his ministry.

How did this humble servant of God come to faith in Christ? Although he was raised in a nominal Orthodox Christian home, he had little interest in spiritual things as a boy, and the Orthodox faith was only so much tradition to him. But the spiritual lights came on for young Bahjet when a missionary teacher came to his school. She carried with her a vibrant faith, and she introduced to Bahjet the truth that he could be born again and could know Jesus personally. Shortly after he prayed to receive Christ, this dear teacher was persecuted by the Orthodox community for introducing the schoolboys to Protestant beliefs. She had to leave the school, but Bahjet's faith remained strong.

So many Christian men I know have similar stories. They came to Christ because of their mother's faith or because of the godly influence of a Sunday school teacher, an aunt or a female neighbor. The great missionary pioneer Hudson Taylor, who helped open up China to the gospel in the mid-1800s, says it was his mother and sister who brought him to a point of true conversion.[1] Evangelist Billy Graham was strongly influenced by the stalwart Presbyterian Bible teacher Henrietta Mears, whose passion for evangelism and discipleship also inspired Bill Bright, founder of Campus Crusade for Christ.[2]

The New Testament provides us a scene in which a female Bible teacher, Priscilla (who had been trained by Paul), offers theological instruction and correction to the man known as Apollos—a fervent disciple who had not been preaching the full gospel of grace. Acts 18:24–28 says that after Priscilla and her husband, Aquila, "explained to him the way of God more accurately" (v. 26), Apollos "powerfully refuted the Jews" by demonstrating that Jesus was the Messiah (v. 28). In this case, a woman's teaching ministry had a profound effect on a man who helped turn the first-century world upside down. I imagine that Apollos forever felt indebted to this godly woman, who was in fact a mentor in his life.

The Bible does not minimize or reject the godly influence of women on the men around them. When Paul wrote to his son in the faith, Timothy, he called him to be grateful for the fact that his mother, Eunice, and his grandmother, Lois, had taught him "genuine faith" (2 Tim. 1:5, NKJV). We don't know where Timothy's father was—perhaps Timothy was raised by these two saintly women. Whatever the case, Paul does not negate or minimize the influence of these women in the life of the young apostle.

We have already examined in chapter eighteen Paul's words to Timothy in which he issued a prohibition of women's teaching. This restriction—which is so often misused as a blanket ban on women in leadership—was obviously limited in its scope because Paul, in other passages of Scripture, allows women to teach and lead. Scholars believe the restriction in 1 Timothy is directed at one of two possible groups:

1. Women who were teaching false doctrines, or
2. Women who were untrained and unprepared for public ministry.

It's important that we look closer at 1 Timothy 2:12:

> But I suffer not a woman to teach, nor to usurp authority over the man, but to be in silence.
>
> —KJV

In their book *I Suffer Not a Woman,* Richard and Catherine Clark Kroeger offer detailed research on the meaning of this Greek word for *usurp,* which is *authentein.* This is the only place in the New Testament where the word is used, leading us to believe that it has a very narrow definition. The word, as it was used in other Greek literature of the day, can sometimes refer to murder, domination and even ritual castration.[3] It does not simply mean "to have authority" as some Bible translations state. The word carries an almost violent connotation.

What was going on in the Ephesian church? The Kroegers' theory is that false teachers who were spreading the dangerous Gnostic heresies of the cult of Diana had invaded the young congregation. In that pagan sect, female priestesses were known to declare women as superior. At the same time they praised Eve as a mother goddess. Some of them were teaching that Eve was the true "author" or "creator" of man! Hence, the Kroegers suggest that 1 Timothy 2:12 could be translated: "I do not allow a woman to teach or proclaim herself author of man."[4]

Such false teaching, of course, would be blasphemous. It contradicts the Bible, twists the order of Creation (by suggesting that woman was made before man) and redefines and overthrows the inherent sexual nature of men and women—an obvious goal of the followers of Diana, who promoted sexual perversion. Certainly God does not allow a woman to usurp a man's role in this way.

However, we cannot use 1 Timothy 2:12 or any other Bible passage to suggest that trained, Spirit-empowered women cannot teach the Scriptures with authority. Nor can we say that women who have been gifted with Spirit-endued giftings of leadership, pastoral anointing or teaching ability must limit their teaching to women only. Men who receive instruction from such women will not be emasculated; on the contrary, they will grow stronger in Christ. It's time for godly male leaders in the church to become secure enough in their manhood to give women a platform.

Question #21
Whom Are You Calling Jezebel?

I've met a lot of strong women who think they are called to church leadership roles. They seem to have a feminist agenda. Don't you think this is harmful to the church?

First of all, let's define what you mean by a *feminist agenda*. In modern American culture, conservative Christians tend to associate feminism with a radical, ungodly set of values that includes legitimizing abortion, gay marriage and homosexual adoption. Many radical feminists who have been elected to political office spend their time fighting wholesome family ideals. Some feminists in the workplace have lobbied for health insurance benefits for the domestic partners of gays and lesbians.

Obviously, these kinds of objectives are unbiblical, and they are unhealthy for any society. This kind of radical feminist agenda isn't good for the corporate world or the political arena, and it certainly doesn't belong in the church. God has never sanctioned homosexuality, and He has never condoned the killing of innocent babies. Nor does He approve of gay activists redefining the family or imposing their sexual liberation agenda on mainstream society.

However, when I hear people talking about a "feminist agenda" in the church, they usually are not referring to someone who is advocating gay marriage or abortion. They tend to use this term to describe a woman who aspires to a leadership position. If she is ambitious, she is automatically labeled a feminist. And that is tragic.

In some conservative Christian circles, any woman who has natural leadership gifts becomes suspect. If she expresses interest in leading a particular committee or ministry, she is labeled "controlling" or "dominating"—even if she has a soft-spoken manner. And if she has a charismatic, aggressive personality, people may label her "power-hungry" or "manipulative." In some churches, a strong woman may even be labeled a "Jezebel"—a very unfair term since the biblical Jezebel was an evil, authoritarian queen who worshiped pagan gods and made eunuchs of God's true prophets.

Perhaps we have forgotten that the feminist movement in the United States actually has Christian roots. It began in the mid-1800s when a group of Quaker and Methodist women—along with some brave pastors and other male supporters—began calling upon society to endow women with the right to vote.

Up until that time, no democratic government in the world gave even marginal civil rights to women. But as a result of the American suffrage movement, women were empowered with far-reaching political freedom. Huge doors of opportunity were opened to them for the first time, and eventually laws were enacted that secured equal pay for equal work. Women were finally protected by law from injustice and discrimination.

These brave leaders of the suffrage movement drew their inspiration from the Scriptures. They believed that the gospel of Christ was the only power in the world that could free women from the curse of cultural oppression and devaluation. They called themselves *feminists* because they believed in restoring to women the dignity that God intended for His daughters.

Many modern feminist leaders have abandoned the godly roots of their original mission. The early pioneers of women's rights— who most certainly opposed abortion and homosexuality—would be horrified if they could see that feminism has degenerated today into a pagan philosophy. Modern feminism is really not feminism at all, since true feminism is the belief that women have God-given rights and human dignity. Many modern feminists have abandoned any mention of religious faith, and some have, in fact, embraced New Age spirituality and goddess worship.

In light of this historical perspective, let's address the question again. Is feminism dangerous to the church? Traditional Christians who ask that question really are asking, "Are strong women dangerous to the church?" or "Shouldn't we be wary of women who seek to be leaders?"

How absurd! The church throughout the centuries has advanced the cause of Christ through the efforts of strong women of faith—and we need more of them. Where would we be today without the fearless women who carried the torch of the gospel in centuries past? Since the day that Jesus' female followers bravely risked their lives to stand beside Him at the cross—and then became the first witnesses of His Resurrection on Easter Sunday—women throughout the centuries have faced incredible opposition to take the gospel to the world.

- The female martyrs of the early church were beheaded, thrown to lions, burned at the stake and raped and mutilated by their Roman oppressors, yet they maintained their testimony for Christ. Some of these women were even forced to watch their own children being tortured and killed, yet they would not recant their faith.

- In the medieval period, courageous mystics like Catherine of Siena withstood imprisonment and criticism from Roman Catholic bishops. Outspoken women such as Joyce Lewes and Joan Waste were burned at the stake by Catholics. (Joan Waste's crime was that she memorized parts of the Bible.)[1]

- In colonial New England, an outspoken woman named Anne Hutchinson dared to criticize the religious control of Puritan leaders. They labeled her a rebel because she believed the Holy Spirit could speak to any Christian. For refusing to renounce her beliefs, she was banished from the Massachusetts Bay Colony and was killed by Indians—becoming the first female Christian martyr in the New World.[2]

- Fearless Quaker women in the late 1700s rode on horseback to preach the gospel from town to town. So did many early followers of John Wesley, the founder of the Methodist movement—and (in the latter part of his life) Wesley himself encouraged women to enter public ministry.

- During the 1800s, countless women missionaries risked death and disease in order to take the gospel to the treacherous mission fields of Africa and Asia. Some of them, like Mary Slessor and Amy Carmichael, blazed a trail for mission work that flourishes today.

- During the Pentecostal revival of the early 1900s, numerous women were "filled with the Holy Spirit" and began establishing churches and organizing revival crusades. Aimee Semple McPherson founded a denomination that as of 2001 claimed more than 3.5 million members.[3]

Brave African American women, including Jerena Lee, had itinerant preaching ministries at a time when blacks had no civil rights.[4]

- In China today, it is estimated that two-thirds of the church planters in the "underground" Protestant church movement are women between the ages of eighteen and twenty-four. Most of these brave young women have been jailed, beaten with iron bars and shocked with electric cattle prods for their faith, but it has not stopped them from aggressively taking ground for Christ. In fact, many missiologists believe that the Chinese are leading more people to Christ today than believers in any other country.

The Bible does not tell us that men should be strong while women should be weak. Weakness is not a feminine virtue. All believers, in fact, are commanded to "be strong in the Lord" (Eph. 6:10). All righteous followers of the Lord are called to be as "bold as a lion" (Prov. 28:1). Women may be weaker in a physical sense than most men, but all of us must heed the words of the Lord to the prophet Joel, who said, "Let the weak say, I am strong" (Joel 3:10, KJV). True strength, after all, is not about muscles or physical prowess, but about determination, resolve, moral courage and zealous faith. Shouldn't women exhibit these qualities?

God is not glorified when a woman is timid, shy or reluctant to speak or act with courage. Timidity is never portrayed as a virtue in the Bible. God has always called His servants, whether male or female, to put their shyness and timidity aside so they can receive supernatural boldness to obey His orders.

Moses was reluctant to speak for God to Pharaoh, but God told him, "I...will be with your mouth, and teach you what you are to say" (Exod. 4:12). In the same way, Esther was afraid to appeal to King Xerxes about the fate of the Jews, but her cousin Mordecai warned her that their deliverance rested on her willingness to risk her life by speaking. So Esther made a conscious decision to leave her comfort zone. She swallowed her fears, called for prayer and fasting to back up her plan and then stepped out in faith to rescue a nation. Her obedience short-circuited an evil conspiracy that was hatched in hell.

It is tragic that the modern church expects Christian women to be demure and passive. This is not God's plan! In some churches, insecure male leaders view strong women as a threat to their position, so they encourage them to stay in the background. This only encourages women to become lazy, materialistic and spiritually bored. It is even worse when insecure women complain about other women who aspire to leadership roles.

On the contrary, the church should be challenging all women to rise up to their high calling in Christ. All women are not called to senior leadership roles, but we should encourage those who have spiritual gifts to develop them—whether those gifts be preaching, teaching, administration, service or showing mercy. And we should be calling all women to become aggressive in evangelism, militant in prayer and bold in their efforts to transform the culture.

Our society is in desperate need of female reformers who will stand up to an ungodly culture. We need fearless women who will proclaim the gospel in the media and in the public square. We need selfless women who will defend the unborn, the orphan, the homeless, the addicted and the victimized. We need compassionate women who are willing to put their own lives at risk to help prostitutes, abused children, drug addicts and runaway teenagers.

Where are the female prophets? Where are the women who will cry out in the streets for justice and compassion? In the Old Testament, God raised up several women who served in powerful positions of authority. Deborah, who judged Israel for more than forty years, was a forerunner of a great company of women who would walk in this realm of authority in the last days. (See Judges 4–5.) Her wise, prophetic counsel on the battlefield resulted in a great military victory and enabled the people of Israel to possess the gates of their enemies.

In Psalm 68:11, we are told that "great is the [company of the women] who bore the tidings" (NRSV, footnote). The psalmist was foreseeing a day in the New Covenant period when women would be released from the oppression of culture, prejudice and religious tradition—so that they could be free to proclaim. This same bright future was seen from a distance by the prophet Joel, who predicted that when the Holy Spirit was poured out on the church, "your sons and daughters will prophesy" (Joel 2:28).

In Proverbs 8, God's wisdom is personified as a woman preacher who stands "beside the gates, at the opening to the city" to call society into account (v. 3). This bold woman shouts her message from the rooftops and demands to be heard. How desperately we need these women preachers to emerge again today.

Yet in today's church, at least in the United States, the majority of Christian women aren't saying anything. We have told women that they should let the men do the leading. We've encouraged them to hide in the shadows. In some churches, women have been virtually gagged and told that the only place they can speak is in the home, at a women's Bible study or to a children's Sunday school class. While those arenas are of great importance, they are not the only places a woman is called to influence.

Why has the church silenced women? Why have we urged them to settle for less? Why have we coaxed them to avoid the spiritual battlefield? I believe the devil is behind this strategy. He knows that there is untapped potential for spiritual revival and reformation when women discover who they are in Christ—and who Christ is in them. He knows that when women receive a divine revelation of their godly authority, God's kingdom will advance and hell will be plundered.

It is time that the church stopped being afraid of strong women. We need them more than ever. We need modern-day Deborahs and Esthers who will hear God's battle strategy and deliver those who are destined to destruction. We need another generation of empowered women who, like the godly suffragists of the late 1800s, will rise up in His might to overcome oppression and leave Christ's mark on society.

More harm will be done to the church by weak women than by strong ones. We need a new generation of women who will emulate the courage of Catherine Booth, Amy Carmichael, Margaret Fell, Frances Willard, Lottie Moon and so many other bold prophetesses from history who did not let their gender tame the fire of God in them.

If you are labeled a *feminist* simply because you decided to step out in faith and obey the call of God on your life, then consider this a minor distraction, and don't let it stop you. In fact, if you continue to pursue a radical call of obedience to God, people will call you worse names. Get used to it. Consider it an honor to lay your reputation on the altar for God's glory.

Question **#22**
Pastors Who
Wear Lipstick

I've attended a church with a woman pastor, and I was appalled by her domineering leadership style. Don't you think women are too controlling and manipulative to be in the role of senior pastor?

A friend recently sent me a list called "Why Men Should Never Be Pastors." This bit of humor included these outrageous statements:

- Men are too emotional to be pastors. Their conduct at football and basketball games proves this.

- Some men are so handsome they will distract women worshipers.

- Their physical build indicates that men are more suited to tasks such as chopping down trees and wrestling mountain lions. It would be "unnatural" for them to do other forms of work.

- The person who betrayed Jesus was a man. Thus, his lack of faith and ensuing punishment stand as a symbol of the subordinate position that all men should take.

- Men are overly prone to violence. No truly masculine man wants to settle disputes without a fight. Thus, men would be poor role models, as well as being dangerously unstable in positions of leadership.

- Ordained pastors are required to nurture their congregations. But this is not a traditional male role. Rather, throughout history, women have been considered more skilled than men at nurturing. This makes them the obvious choice for ordination.

- For men who have children, their pastoral duties might distract them from the responsibility of being a parent.

- Men can still be involved in church activities, even without being ordained. They can sweep sidewalks, repair the church roof and maybe even lead the singing on Father's Day. By confining themselves to such traditional male roles, they can still be vitally important in the life of the church.

Obviously the author of this anonymous bit of humor was poking fun at the excuses people have invented to keep women out of the ministry. I've heard all of these excuses—and many more—from both men and women who are uncomfortable with women preachers and pastors. But the one excuse that outshines them all is the one you have mentioned. It is the excuse that says: "Women shouldn't pastor because I knew a woman pastor once, and she did a terrible job."

Did you ever know a male pastor who was a poor communicator in the pulpit? Did you assume that since he could not speak very well in public, all men are weak preachers? Of course not.

Did you ever know a male pastor who had serious flaws? Did you ever read about a male minister who embezzled money from his church, committed adultery with his secretary or abused his power in some way? Because of these men's mistakes, did you therefore assume that all male ministers are corrupt and therefore ineligible for ordination?

During the time that I have been editor of *Charisma* magazine, I've had to report on some of the most embarrassing scandals in recent church history. One California pastor divorced his wife, married another woman after just seven days, and then was back in the pulpit the next week enjoying the applause of his gullible congregation. Another prominent television evangelist lied about a major fund-raising effort, then had an affair with his secretary, got her pregnant, divorced his wife and married the younger woman. Another popular traveling minister carried on a homosexual affair with the youth pastor of his church until it was uncovered and hit the local newspaper.

All of these incidents triggered embarrassing national scandals and caused many of those who followed these men to become disillusioned with church leadership in general. A similar tragedy occurred in the Roman Catholic Church when the media uncovered a painful pattern of priests engaging in child sexual abuse. Among Catholics in the pews, the level of confidence in clergy has sunk to an all-time low—not only because innocent children had been violated by men of the cloth, but also because their male bishops looked the other way and refused to discipline these wayward priests.

Yet with all of these mistakes among men who claimed to represent God, no one dares to say it is because of their gender. Why is it, then, that when a woman assumes a leadership role in the church—or even in society at large—we are so quick to blame her faults on her femininity? There are three reasons we do this.

Deeply Ingrained Gender Prejudice

Even after women gained the right to vote in 1920 and achieved economic rights in the workplace in the 1960s and 1970s, our culture still struggles with gender bias and stereotyping. Just as racism has been slow to die, degrading attitudes about women still abound in our culture—and in the church. Among conservative evangelical Christians, many people—both men and women—hold a view that says women are emotionally weak, incapable of handling pressure or stress, too talkative, too manipulative, indecisive, unintelligent and unpredictable because of hormonal mood swings. Yet all of these are stereotypes.

It is true that some women are manipulative. It is certainly true that some women are indecisive. But these qualities have nothing to do with their gender. I know men who are so indecisive they haven't been able to take the risks necessary to start a successful career, get married and start a family. I also know men who are manipulative, overly emotional, petty and talkative—all qualities that are stereotypically applied to women.

In the church, our gender prejudices have actually been canonized by popular evangelical literature. Some Christian books have focused on explaining male and female "biblical roles," but often the concepts presented in these books are nothing more than gender stereotypes. We are told that typical men "bury their emotions," as if this is a healthy quality, while women are "nurturers by nature," as if men are not called to be loving and nurturing as well. Men are "aggressive," while women are supposed to be "passive." (Meanwhile, the Bible calls all believers to be filled with God's Spirit and aggressively engaged in His bold mission to reach the world for Christ.)

These books also claim that God made men to be "leaders"

while He fashioned women to be "followers." Wayne Grudem and John Piper, two well-known seminarians, dismiss the prophet Deborah's leadership skills by saying that God really never intended for her to assume that senior position in the first place. Their theory is that Deborah would never have been a prophet if Barak had been a more courageous leader, as men are supposed to be. Since Deborah did not fit into these evangelical authors' list of male/female stereotypes, they cut her out of their Bible altogether.[1]

Misapplied Scriptures

Many Christians have been taught that one verse in the Bible, 1 Timothy 2:12 ("I do not allow a woman to teach or exercise authority over a man"), prevents women in all situations and at all times from serving as pastors or elders. I looked more closely at this passage in chapter eighteen. For the sake of brevity, let me state here that this verse must be read in context with all of the New Testament. And when we read it in context, we must face the fact that Paul encouraged women to teach. He had women teachers and leaders on his traveling apostolic team, and he mentions several women who obviously carried the weight of church authority. Therefore, 1 Timothy 2:12 cannot be used as a blanket prohibition of women teachers or leaders.

Three women mentioned in Paul's epistles are obvious reminders that the same apostle who wrote 1 Timothy 2:12 (in order to correct a situation that involved dangerous false teaching) did, in fact, install women to lead churches. Besides the obvious teaching and leadership provided by Priscilla (Acts 18:24–28) and the deacon known as Phoebe (Rom. 16:1–2), Paul mentioned the woman Nympha, who had a church in her house in Laodicia (Col. 4:15). Did Nympha pastor the church? Most likely, but modern evangelicals—who have no room in their religious mind-sets for a female shepherd—dismiss her by assuming that she was either "hosting" the church like an administrator or perhaps paying its bills and protecting it from government harassment as a "patron."

Paul also mentioned two other female church leaders in Philippians 4:2–3:

> I plead with Euodia and I plead with Syntyche to agree with each other in the Lord. Yes, and I ask you, loyal yokefellow, help these women who have contended at my side in the cause of the gospel.
>
> —NIV

We are given no clue as to what kind of disagreement had broken fellowship between Euodia and Syntyche. All we know is that their disunity was of great concern for Paul, since he obviously loved both of them as sisters who had worked with him faithfully. Although their exact roles are not specified here, the fact that they labored by Paul's side most likely indicates that they were engaged in church planting and discipleship ministry. It is possible that they pastored multiple congregations or even shared oversight for them. The fact that they had broken fellowship troubled Paul because he himself had experienced painful breaks with workers in the past.

One thing is certain: Paul's response to Euodia and Syntyche was not to throw them out of the ministry simply because they were women. Nor did he hand down an edict banning women from leadership just because these two gifted female ministers got into an argument.

A Lack of Female Role Models

One reason women pastors and church leaders are so quickly judged today is because there aren't as many positive examples of women ministers. We still have a long way to go, and people are still getting used to the idea that women can successfully lead churches. Today, a group of brave women are blazing a trail for their sisters to come behind them, and they will most likely encounter many more years of resistance before it becomes accepted in the church. They need some brave men to come alongside them and champion their cause.

It does not help that there have indeed been some bad examples of women ministers. Back in the early 1990s, I reported on a growing Hispanic church in Texas that was pastored by a woman. She was breaking new ground for women in leadership, or so I thought. But a few years later, I learned that her church had dwindled because she had an abusive leadership style (which she learned, sadly, from her male mentors). Rather than leading her congregation in a Christlike way with humility and kindness, she took on a demanding tone and a forceful, autocratic style. Thus she drove the sheep away rather than attracting them to the healing power of Christ.

Ministers of the gospel are required to be gentle, peaceable, hospitable and prudent (1 Tim. 3:2–3). That same passage says that leaders in the church must not be pugnacious or given to anger. Controlling, domineering leadership styles have no place in God's church—in either men or women leaders. Jesus told us that if we truly desire to lead, we must be servants. This is the posture that is required of every female who says *yes* to the call of God.

Of the many women I meet who are called to leadership, some of them are what I call axe-grinders. They obviously have spiritual giftings to preach or lead people, but they also carry an attitude. For some, it is the "I'll show you" attitude. These women are out to prove that they can do the same job a man can do, and they take on an arrogant, bitter spirit in the process.

Others have a "You'd better listen to me" attitude. They think that because they are called by God, they can push people around and demand obedience. Rather than entreating the saints with a gracious spirit, they become hard and insensitive. They eventually develop a dictatorial leadership style. And they end up repelling the very people they are called to serve and encourage.

These axe-grinders and dictators are not helping the cause of women in ministry. They would do us all a favor if they would step aside and allow humble, broken women to take their places in leadership.

I met some of these broken women when I visited with a group of leaders of China's underground church in January 2001. I met at least twenty-five top female leaders of the underground church during that visit, and all of them had spent at least a year or more in jail because of their illegal evangelistic activities. Some of them had been beaten with iron rods. Others had been shocked continually with electric cattle prods. Others had been forced to spend long winters sleeping on cold concrete prison floors—with no sweaters, warm clothes or feminine hygiene products. Yet all of these women were excited about taking the gospel to the villages of China!

One night, after I had ministered in one of the meetings with these leaders, I went back to my hotel room and found two of these women standing at my door, waiting with another woman who had volunteered to translate. The translator told me that the women wanted me to pray for them because they did not receive ministry at the altar during the meeting.

"Are you pastors or evangelists?" I asked them.

"Yes," they answered with a smile.

"How many churches do you oversee?" I then asked.

The first woman answered, "Two thousand."

The second woman answered, "Five thousand."

I was stunned. These women had spiritual responsibility for

more churches than most men I know who are involved in church planting in the United States. Yet they were humble women who simply had a passion to serve the Lord and to see Him move in miraculous ways. I felt unqualified to minister to these heroes of the underground church, but I honored their request.

After I prayed for them that evening, I realized that if they came to the United States, we probably would not allow them to preach in our churches on a Sunday morning. And we would certainly not allow them to start a new church or pastor a congregation that they started—even though they could probably teach the seminary class on church planting! I suppose that in China, the Holy Spirit is moving so fast that no one has time to control the process or to question how God is using the sisters. And because there are so many effective women in ministry in China, it has become accepted for them to do what many of us still consider to be non-traditional.

It is time for us to take our cue from the Chinese church, where more than twenty-five thousand people come to faith in Christ every day. Perhaps if we release our sisters to pastor and preach, we will move closer to seeing the same level of revival and church growth that the underground Chinese church has seen during the past twenty years.

Question #23
The Stigma of Divorce

My church says I can't serve in any type of ministry role because I've been divorced. My marriage ended twenty years ago. Is it true that I should be branded "unusable" because of my marital failure?

Over the years I've met many men and women who've experienced painful rejection from their Christian friends after their marriages ended. This might be understandable if the person had committed adultery and was unrepentant. But often the innocent party in a divorce is also shunned or ostracized by his or her own congregation, as if the status of divorce itself is a form of leprosy. Or a person who made mistakes and ruined a marriage years ago is made to feel they must pay for their failure for the rest of their lives. Hope for recovery and restoration is often the last thing we offer them. We might as well brand them with a scarlet D and lock them in a set of stocks in the churchyard. It's no wonder that so many divorced people give up on the church altogether!

I met a woman who was a faithful member of a Pentecostal church in Illinois. She had been a model member of the congregation, but the church turned against her when her husband left her for another woman. Even though the divorce occurred because of her husband's unfaithfulness, she bore the guilt. It was assumed that she must have caused the marriage to end—therefore she must suffer. One day her pastor called to inform her that she could no longer participate in any visible ministry at the church. No more singing in the choir, playing the piano or greeting visitors. Divorce had disqualified her.

This may seem extreme, but it happens more often than we realize in conservative churches. There are many divorced Christians today who feel they've been banished to a living form of purgatory. And it's even worse when the people involved are ministers.

For example, consider the pastor who came home one day and discovered that his wife had left him and moved all the furniture out of the house. In desperation he called a Christian "divorce care" hotline for pastors because he didn't want to tell his denomination the news. He knew that he could lose his church, his income, his health insurance and his reputation overnight—even though he did not initiate the divorce and had not been unfaithful to his wife.

A gifted pastor and Bible teacher who was ordained in a Pentecostal denomination learned one dreary afternoon that his wife had been having an affair with another man. Although the pastor was devastated to hear his wife's confession, he was open to working things out and staying in the marriage. But his wife was cold and unresponsive to his expressions of forgiveness, and she announced that it was over.

When the divorce was final, the pastor knew he faced some tough choices. Even though the failure of his marriage was not his fault, his denomination's ordination policy stated that no minister who gets a divorce can remain credentialed if he remarries.

Variations of this policy are enforced today by many denominations. The message is clear: If you have been divorced and remarried, don't apply for ministerial status. You've struck out.

But is it biblical to automatically disqualify a divorced minister and never allow him to return to the pulpit—even if he or she submits to counseling, accountability and a program of restoration?

This no-divorced-pastors policy—which is common in many denominations—is loosely based on the apostle Paul's qualifications for elders, listed in 1 Timothy 3:7. Aside from requiring male elders in 1 Timothy 3:7 to "have a good reputation with those outside the church" (which could feasibly apply to the issue of divorce if a man's treatment of his wife was scandalous), Paul said a leader "must be...the husband of one wife" (v. 2). The same phrase is also repeated in Titus 1:6 in a similar list of qualifications for elders. Paul also required that women who aspire to be a part of the order of widows (a class of female church workers) must have been "the wife of one man" (1 Tim. 5:9). And he required female elders, in 1 Timothy 3:11, to be "faithful" and "temperate in all things"—which would certainly apply to her marital relationship.

Many churches interpret 1 Timothy 3:7 to mean that a divorced and remarried man actually has two spouses and is therefore disqualified. But is that really what the text is saying?

Bible scholars certainly do not agree. Some believe Paul is referring to polygamy. In other words, if a man has two or more wives at home, he doesn't qualify to lead the church. Polygamy certainly was practiced in parts of the Middle East during New Testament times, although it was against Roman law. Theologian Craig Keener points out that rabbis in Palestine sometimes allowed a man to have up to eighteen wives![1]

Others believe "husband of one wife" requires elders to be

married—thereby disqualifying bachelors or widowers. (Such a policy, then, would actually require a divorced man to remarry.) Still other scholars have suggested that the phrase "husband of one wife" can be interpreted to mean "a one-woman man"— suggesting that elders should simply exhibit sexual faithfulness to their current wife. The same could apply to women in 1 Timothy 5:9. Paul's directive here could mean that a widow could not qualify for a ministry position unless she had exhibited marital faithfulness while her husband was alive.

Craig Keener, in his excellent book...*And Marries Another,* suggests that what Paul was requiring among leaders in 1 Timothy 3:7 was simply marital faithfulness and sexual integrity in their current lifestyle—not some kind of proof that they never made a mistake in a past relationship. If this were true, then a divorced man who has remarried and who exhibits faithfulness in his current marriage (with no mistresses or concubines on the side) would qualify for a ministerial position.

This view would certainly be consistent with the Bible's message of redemption. Christ came to cleanse us from the sins of our past and to give us new life. After all, why would He choose to forgive all our past mistakes except those involving divorce? What about blasphemy? Paul persecuted the early Christians and endorsed the martyrdom of Stephen, yet his actions did not disqualify him from serving as an apostle. Peter betrayed Jesus by denying Him three times, yet this did not disqualify him from his office.

Redemption made the difference for Peter and Paul. And it is the same message of redemption and healing that we must offer today to those whose lives have been wrecked by divorce— especially people who have suffered judgment and mistreatment even though they were the innocent parties in a divorce. Says Keener:

God, who knows the hearts of us all, will ultimately
vindicate or condemn; but His church, if it errs,
must err on the side of mercy rather than of judgment. Paul allows for the existence and remarriage
of an innocent party, and it is time that many
Christians today learn to do the same.[2]

If you are divorced, or divorced and remarried, and you feel a
call to some level of ministry, you need to be aware that some
churches and denominations do have strict policies that may
limit your involvement.

- The Assemblies of God, for example, will allow a
  divorced person to be ordained, but not a person who
  has been divorced and remarried (unless the remarriage
  occurred before salvation).

- Southern Baptist churches are autonomous, therefore
  each church makes its own decisions about pastoral can-
  didates. But as a rule, the Southern Baptist Convention
  (SBC) frowns on ordaining divorced and remarried per-
  sons because of the 1 Timothy 3:7 rule. Also, the SBC's
  foreign mission board will not appoint a divorced person
  as a missionary. (Note also that the SBC does not ordain
  women to be pastors.)

- The Church of God (Cleveland, Tennessee) will credential
  a divorced minister if he or she can prove that the marriage ended because of the infidelity of the former spouse.

- The International Church of the Foursquare Gospel
  (whose founder, Aimee Semple MacPherson, was divorced
  twice) ordains divorced people, but it appoints an ethics
  committee to look at each individual case.

- Many independent charismatic church networks do not have a blanket prohibition against ordaining divorced ministers. Meanwhile, no specific policy has been enacted to restrict divorced ministers in the United Methodist Church or the Presbyterian Church (U.S.A.).[3] (And traditionalists conclude that the lax policy on divorce in these mainline groups has encouraged theological drift.)

If you feel you are called to pursue ordination or some level of ministry status, it is not likely that you are going to change an existing policy in your lifetime. It would be better for you to change your denominational affiliation and pursue the doors that are open to you.

You will likely encounter rejection and criticism from well-intentioned religious people. That's why your priority must be to appropriate all the healing God offers you. There is hope for total recovery after divorce. You can be freed from all of its rejection and hurts. You do not have to live with a dark cloud over your head or a scarlet D around your neck. Discover His healing, and consider joining a divorce recovery group at a healthy church so you can surround yourself with the support of friends who understand your unique dilemma.

Genuine, compassionate ministry will flow from you when you have put the wounds and failures of the past behind you. And because you understand the pain of divorce and have suffered its stigma—God will use you to offer mercy, restoration and grace to divorced people who have been wrongly judged as unfit for the kingdom.

Question #24
Tough Choices

What if a woman feels called to ministry, but her church or denomination doesn't allow women to teach or to serve in certain positions. What should she do?

It is always difficult when we are thrust into a situation in which church leaders ask us to do one thing yet we feel called by God to do the opposite. Do we obey church authorities no matter what, even if what they are requiring conflicts with biblical principles? Or is it ever right to disobey their directives?

There is definitely a time and place to defy orders. When the chief priests and rabbinical leaders of Jerusalem commanded Peter and the apostles to stop their preaching, Peter told them, "We cannot stop speaking what we have seen and heard" (Acts 4:20). The priests, who were blinded by their own religious traditions, interpreted the disciples' behavior as flagrant insubordination to God. The early apostles had to get used to being called rebels. You too may be required to wear this label if you intend to step out into a ministry calling.

Let's remember the Hebrew midwives, Shiphrah and Puah.

Egypt's pharaoh told them to kill every male infant born to the Hebrew slaves, but these cunningly wise women figured out a way to get around the law. The Scriptures tell us that they "feared God, and did not do as the king of Egypt had commanded them" (Exod. 1:17). When he confronted them after learning that baby boys were still being born in Goshen, Shiphrah and Puah invented an elaborate excuse—saying that the slave women gave birth too quickly. Apparently Pharaoh believed their alibi and did not punish them.

This is what I call *holy shrewdness*. Sometimes God allows us to be sneaky. Theologians might claim that it is wrong for people to lie for godly reasons, but it is obvious from the Exodus account that God blessed the cleverness of these midwives. Had Shiphrah and Puah not disobeyed the pharaoh's edict, countless Hebrew boys would have been slaughtered by Egyptian daggers.

Many other women in Scripture had to employ this cunning. The harlot Rahab defied the edict given by the rulers of Jericho. Because she hid the Hebrew spies on her roof and lied in order to protect them, her life was spared. She eventually joined the Israelites and embraced their faith in the true God. And God gave her the ultimate honor by having her listed in the lineage of Christ (Matt. 1:5).

The maiden Esther tricked Haman into coming to her banquet so she could expose his murderous plot in front of King Xerxes. She also defied the laws and customs of the palace by approaching the throne without being summoned, knowing that the king could have ordered her instant execution or banishment. Her God-given concern for the Lord's people pushed her to break the rules.

Are you willing to defy authorities when you know you have truth on your side? Corrie ten Boom, the famous Dutch survivor of the Holocaust, carried out an elaborately deceptive plan to hide Jews in her father's house during the Nazi occupation of Holland.

She and her family built their famous "hiding place" for Jews in an upstairs bedroom by concealing building materials inside grandfather clocks and milk bottles. Yet Corrie's own pastor disagreed with her strategy, suggesting that she shouldn't disobey the government. In the end, Corrie survived the hell of a German prison camp—and her story of faith and forgiveness has led thousands of people to Christ. If Corrie had accepted her pastor's advice, countless Jews would not have been spared, her testimony would never have touched the world, and she most likely would have been haunted by a guilty conscience.

Just before the war on terrorism began in 2001, two unknown female missionaries from the United States—Heather Mercer and Dayna Curry—disobeyed the strict laws of Afghanistan by showing a gospel video on their laptop computer to a Muslim family in Kabul. They were arrested, along with six other colleagues from their mission base. After the September 11 terrorist attacks, these two women and their teammates found themselves in a crude Taliban prison while American troops and their allies were invading Afghanistan. Amazingly, they lived to tell about the ordeal—after spending three and one-half months in unsanitary conditions while bombs exploded all around them.

When *Charisma* magazine asked Heather Mercer if she would do it all over again, she didn't hesitate to say *yes*. "Prison was the greatest privilege of my life—God's blessing to me," she said. "We had the privilege of being a part of God's changing history in Afghanistan. I wouldn't trade it for the world."[1] What would have happened if Heather and Dayna had not defied Afghan law? We may never know for sure. But some Christians have theorized that many more Christians around the world focused their prayers on Afghanistan in late 2002 because of the plight of these imprisoned missionaries. It is possible that the presence of Heather Mercer,

Dayna Curry and the other members of the Shelter Now mission who were in that Afghan jail turned history around and opened up an entire nation to the gospel.

I'm grateful, personally, for women who don't always obey the rules. When I was a senior in high school I attended a Southern Baptist church in the Atlanta area. My Sunday school teacher, a middle-aged woman named June, had been told by our pastor never to talk about her experience with the Holy Spirit. The pastor felt this woman was "too radical" in her faith—because she had a dynamic prayer life, she heard God speak to her and sometimes she even spoke in tongues. Because our denominational traditions did not endorse Pentecostal phenomena, the pastor asked June never to talk about them in the Sunday school class.

June was partially obedient, at least in the sense that she did not talk about the "forbidden" topics during the class itself. But when I inquired about her relationship with the Holy Spirit, she recognized that I had a genuine hunger to know more. So she invited a friend and me to her home for an afternoon discussion.

After I heard her share more from the Scriptures about these contraband doctrines, I wanted to experience the Holy Spirit's fullness even more. Within a few weeks, I too was labeled a "rebel." My life was radically transformed after my own encounter with the Holy Spirit—and I have a woman named June to thank for that. To this day I thank God regularly that she did not obey the orders of her pastor.

Guidelines for Consideration

I don't know your specific situation. Perhaps your pastor has told you that you will never be allowed to teach from the pulpit of your church. Perhaps you have been told that women will never serve as elders or deacons in your congregation. Perhaps you've expressed an interest in going to seminary or entering the pastorate, and your denomination has tried to steer you away from this plan because "women can't be pastors." There are no pat answers to solve such dilemmas, but these guidelines will be helpful:

1. Don't allow yourself to become bitter or critical.

Never take it personally when a church leader tries to restrict your ministry or your calling. If he is motivated by gender prejudice or by a limited doctrinal position, then you must have compassion on him. Pray for him regularly, and ask God to bless him. Carefully watch your heart so that a root of bitterness does not spring up. If Satan can tempt you to harbor unforgiveness, then he can derail your ministry.

I've met many women who felt called to ministry, but because they allowed an offense to grow in their hearts they became hardened and cynical. They began to view everything in life through the lens of their hurt. Even their demeanor became hard, angry and insensitive. God cannot use a person who is bitter, so don't even go there! You must reflect the love of Christ in your response to injustice or prejudice.

2. Ask the Holy Spirit for His direction.

You have legitimate questions that need to be answered. Should you leave your church since they have rules that restrict women? Or is God perhaps calling you to stay so that you can influence the situation from the inside? Does God want you to be involved in some "holy shrewdness"? He may even want you to stay so that you can confront the leaders, in a loving way, with Scripture.

You will never be certain what you should do until you surrender completely to God's will. Tell God you will obey Him, no matter the cost. Tell Him you will stay or go. Then watch and wait for His signals. God will make it clear by speaking to you—either through circumstances, through a Scripture, through the counsel of others or by hearing His voice during prayer.

3. Don't place too much importance on the approval of church leaders.

People who aspire to enter the ministry must have a humble spirit, and we should never treat church leaders in a disrespectful manner. But at the same time we cannot elevate leaders higher than God Himself. I know some women who are stifling their gifts and callings because they don't want to rock the boat. They don't want pastors or other respectable people in the church to think of them as being "out of order" or "troublemakers."

But guess what? If you are a woman called to ministry, you are going to make trouble. You are going to upset religious people on a regular basis. Get used to it. You cannot care too much about what people think. The Bible says that the fear of man brings a snare (Prov. 29:25). You will find yourself trapped and immobilized if you place too much value in other people's opinions of you. And no woman trapped in this snare will do anything worthwhile for God.

Billy Graham's daughter Anne Graham Lotz appeared on the *Larry King Live* program in 2001 to talk about her father and about her own ministry. When King asked her if she worried about upsetting Southern Baptist leaders (who do not endorse women in senior leadership positions), Lotz fired back, "Larry, I don't believe I am accountable to them."

Anne understands an important principle of ultimate accountability. You too must understand that you are first and foremost accountable to God for the spiritual gifts He has entrusted to you. If you bury them just because a pastor told you to be quiet, will God accept that as a valid excuse?

4. If you leave your church, keep a positive and loving attitude toward those who rejected you.

I know many women who had to leave their denomination eventually because their ministries were not recognized. One woman was told she could not be a pastor in the Church of God in Christ, the largest black Pentecostal denomination in the United States. So she joined a denomination that does ordain women, and today she has a two-thousand-member church in Virginia that is transforming the inner city and reaching drug addicts, single moms and underprivileged youth.

I know another woman in the Church of God in Christ who employed a bit of holy shrewdness to find her place in the ministry. She asked her father, who was a bishop in the denomination, to ordain her—even though this was against the rules. He defied the presiding bishop's board and ordained his daughter because he believed he was right and they were wrong. Eventually his daughter's church became highly successful even though the elders of the denomination no longer welcomed her into their fold. And she never spoke a negative word against the men who rejected her.

If you move on, God's blessing will move with you as long as you continue to trust Him. But don't curse the people who opposed you. Don't speak ill of those who didn't recognize your gifts. At least they gave you a foundation to build upon. Keep the lines of communication open to those who rejected you. One day they may ask for reconciliation.

5. Make sure you surround yourself with godly counselors and mentors.

Don't allow yourself to have an independent spirit. This can be a serious temptation, especially if people you have trusted in ministry end up betraying you. But if you don't stay humble, you are setting yourself up for a troublesome fall later. Pride will always lead you down the wrong path.

Today there are many places for displaced women ministers to find healthy support. You may have to go outside your denominational tradition to find it, but that will provide you with an opportunity to grow and meet people from other streams in the body of Christ. Allow them to speak into your life.

I highly recommend that all women who feel called to ministry join Christians for Biblical Equality (CBE), an evangelical organization that exists to promote reformation in the church and greater acceptance of women in ministry. Supported by Bible scholars and notable Christian leaders (both men and women), CBE provides conferences, an online bookstore, a quarterly journal called *Priscilla Papers* and other resources for people who share this passion to empower women for service. (Write CBE, 122 West Franklin Ave., Suite 218, Minneapolis, MN 55404, or go online to www.cbeinternational.org.)

Don't ever think you are alone in your struggle. There are many men and women in the church today who understand your dilemma and who want to come alongside you to help. You need their encouragement as well as their instruction and loving correction.

Question #25
Don't Give Up on the Church

I have quit going to church because the leaders are so prejudiced against women. They won't let us serve in any capacity, so why bother? Is there hope that the church will change its views?

For centuries, women have put up with all kinds of prejudice and injustice in the church. The truth is that women in previous generations faced much tougher obstacles, yet the bleakness of their circumstances only seemed to give them more courage and stamina to keep going. They challenged the system, and they persevered, often paying an enormous price. Some even gave their lives.

They kept the faith. So why shouldn't you—especially since you actually have it much easier than they did? You need to take inspiration from the lives of those who have gone before us. The history of the church is full of examples of brave women who held on to hope even when they faced mammoth challenges.

One of the most courageous missionaries ever to be sent out from the United States was Amanda Smith (1837–1915), an African American woman who was born a slave in Maryland. The odds were stacked against her in every way: She had no civil rights because of her race, plus she was a woman—yet she felt a strong call to preach the gospel even though black denominations in her day were not open to women ministers. Her life was almost ruined by poverty, social injustice and two difficult marriages. Four of her five children died in infancy. The emotional toll of such loss probably would have stopped most of us from pursuing any kind of dream.

When Amanda launched out into full-time evangelistic work in 1870, she had to supplement her income by washing and ironing clothes. Yet she kept on believing that God had called her, and her unusual anointing in the pulpit opened up doors for her in churches and revivalist camp meetings. Notable Christian leaders of her day acknowledged that she had an exceptional preaching gift. Eventually, opportunities opened for her to take her holiness message to England, and this led to missionary journeys to India and Liberia, where she worked for eight years before illness forced her to return to the United States. After coming home, she opened the first orphanage for underprivileged black girls in the state of Illinois.[1]

People who opposed the concept of women's ordination criticized Amanda—even though she actually never sought to be ordained. (She wrote in her autobiography, in fact, that ordination never entered her mind because she believed that God alone had ordained her when He called her to preach.)[2]

Amanda faced constant opposition from both blacks and whites who referred to her in a derogatory way as "preacher woman." When she was speaking in England, a group of leaders from the Plymouth Brethren followed her around in order to discredit her. She said of that incident, "The work seemed to be signally blessed of God. But the good Plymouth brethren did not see it at all, because I was a woman; not that I was a black woman, but a woman . . . They would try, in a nice way, to get me into an argument; but I always avoided anything of the kind."[3]

The Brethren even launched an attack on Amanda in the newspapers, and they bombarded her with letters containing "scriptural texts against women preaching."[4] But those texts, so often misused to squelch a woman's spiritual gifts, did not stop her from venturing to Asia and Africa. God seemed to pave the way before her, confirming her message and supplying her financial needs.

Another courageous woman minister who overcame incredible odds was Mary McLeod Bethune (1875–1955), a daughter of South Carolina slaves who learned to read in a missionary school and eventually won a scholarship to Moody Bible Institute in Chicago. While a student there, she developed a strong sense of calling to the mission field, but when she applied for an assignment in Africa she was told, in a letter of rejection, "There are no openings in Africa for black missionaries."[5]

Imagine the sense of injustice she must have felt—to be told by white men that she was not qualified to be a missionary to her own race! Mary never went overseas, but she founded a mission school in Daytona Beach, Florida—and some of her graduates did go to Africa as ministers. Meanwhile, she became known as a champion against oppression, especially after she confronted local Ku Klux Klan members who had planned to stage a raid in order to stop blacks from voting. Her courage brought her so much notoriety that Eleanor Roosevelt appointed her to head a federal agency.

If you read the history of missions, you cannot ignore the remarkable contributions made by women who dared to challenge the status quo. They faced enormous opposition, yet they plowed ahead and ignored their critics. American missionary Malla Moe (1863–1954), for example, served in South Africa for sixty-one years, working for the Scandinavian Alliance Mission. On the field she preached, discipled new converts and planted churches—yet when she visited churches in Norway to report on her work, she was not permitted to speak. Church officials "reminded her to read Paul's instruction that 'women should keep silence in the church.'" [6]

Can you imagine the humiliation? Malla had established numerous congregations, led worship services and brought hundreds of men and women to faith in Christ overseas, but when she stepped onto the soil of the mother church she was expected to put her spiritual gifts on a shelf. This double standard is still quite common today. As irrational as it sounds, many churches allow women to participate fully in ministry if it is overseas, but the women are expected to abide by another set of religious rules when they return on furlough.

This is Phariseeism in its worst form. But any woman who wants to be used by God should prepare to face the Pharisees on a regular basis. Jesus promised that we would be persecuted, and often the worst persecution comes from religious people.

What is amazing about Amanda Smith, Mary McLeod Bethune and Malla Moe is that they did not give up when they were confronted with prejudice and injustice. The Holy Spirit gave them the grace to forgive and to continue pressing forward. Women in the church today need a fresh baptism of this tenacity.

Please don't quit. Giving up on the church is not an option for anyone. You may feel discouraged, but you can't just throw in the towel and stop believing. That's what the devil would love for you to do. No matter how many obstacles you face or how bleak the circumstances may seem, faith will pave the way for a victory if you persevere.

God's ultimate plan is to spread the gospel of Jesus Christ through His church, and He does not have a "Plan B" if the church doesn't fulfill its mission. God will have His way, and He will make sure that His church prevails before Christ's return. You can have hope because there are some very special promises in God's Word about the role of women and how they will be used in the last days of the church age. Let me remind you of these promises.

The Promise of Female Prophets

Long before women ever gained any significant degree of social acceptance or civil rights, the prophet Joel foretold of a day when both men and women would speak for God and carry His anointing. This promise, recorded in the Book of Joel, was repeated by the apostle Peter in his inaugural gospel sermon on the Day of Pentecost. That promise says:

> And it will come about after this that I will pour out My Spirit on all mankind; and your sons *and daughters* will prophesy, your old men will dream dreams, your young men will see visions. And even on the male *and female* servants I will pour out My Spirit in those days.
>
> —JOEL 2:28–29, EMPHASIS ADDED

This was a revolutionary concept in Joel's day. It foretold of a time when God's Spirit would not be restricted to the few. It pointed to the age of the church, when the word of the Lord would be accessible to rich and poor, old and young, male and female, Jew and Gentile. And it specifically mentions—twice—that women will be among those who prophesy. It points to a day when women in mass numbers will crisscross the globe, heralding the Good News.

This promise was fulfilled in the first century when women including Phoebe, Priscilla, Junia and Nympha (all mentioned in Paul's epistles) carried the gospel to the Roman Empire. It was fulfilled in even greater measure in the second and third centuries, when women such as Blandina and Perpetua were martyred by

Roman authorities for preaching the message that Christ, not Caesar, was Lord of all. And Joel 2:28 was fulfilled in an even greater measure in the 1800s, when an army of European women responded to the Great Commission to take the gospel to Asia and Africa.

What about the twenty-first century? I believe the prophet's promise will have its most significant fulfillment in our generation, as women in every region of the world are more fully equipped and released to prophesy.

The Promise of a "Great Company" of Women Ministers

Psalm 68:11 is a curious verse, because it is worded so differently in various translations. The New International Version says, "The Lord announced the word, and great was the company of those who proclaimed it." Yet scholars concede that it should be translated this way:

> God giveth the Word: the women that publish the tidings are a great host.[7]

Once again, we have an Old Testament promise that one day a great company of women will be involved in the proclamation of God's truth. When this psalm was written, women were bought and sold like property and treated like animals. Yet David, by the Holy Spirit's inspiration, saw a glorious day ahead when male and female alike would be set free into the glorious liberty of the children of God so that they might inherit His covenant blessings and carry His gospel worldwide.

Notice that this verse says that *God gives the word*. This emerging, End-Time company of women ministers will not be sent by men or commissioned by their own power or ability. They will not go out with their own agenda, nor will their ordination be the result of a political or social movement. It is a work of God. He will open the doors for them, and He will send them with His power. And no man or religious tradition will be able to stop it.

The Promise of Victory to Woman's "Seed"

In the Genesis account of man's fall into sin, we are told that God cursed the serpent and then warned him of his ultimate fate—which was curiously linked to the woman whom the devil had deceived. God said to Satan:

> And I will put enmity between you and the woman,
> and between your seed and her seed; He shall bruise
> you on the head, and you shall bruise him on the heel.
>
> —GENESIS 3:15

This, the first prophecy in the Bible, represents the glorious promise that one day a Messiah would come to earth, born of a virgin, and strip the devil of all his power. And because God planned to use a frail teenage girl (the Virgin Mary) to bring forth the promised Deliverer, the Bible says an unusual hostility would be aimed at women by Satan's forces.

This has certainly been the case. Since the Garden of Eden, Satan has targeted women. In every culture on this planet they have endured untold oppression, injustice and abuse. Why? Because the devil fears what they might do to him. If the Virgin Mary could give birth to Jesus Christ and destroy the kingdom of darkness, what will an army of women—overshadowed by the miraculous power of the Spirit—do to his demonic forces in this hour?

Argentinean evangelist Ed Silvoso likes to call women "God's secret weapons." He suggests that Satan fears what women will one day do to him:

The devil knows that God does not lie—what God promises always comes to pass. This is why Satan has spent centuries belittling women and weaving a web of lies into a formidable worldwide network of oppression to hold them down. He knows that when women find out who they really are, his evil kingdom will come to an abrupt end. He cannot afford to have women walking upright. He desperately needs to keep them down.[8]

This is God's perfect vengeance. The woman who was deceived by the devil will one day be instrumental in his ultimate defeat. Perhaps God has reserved women for the last grand battle with the dragon. Scripture is clear that Jesus crushed the serpent's head. In the same way, the ministries that come forth from anointed women in the End-Times church will drive a spike through Satan's skull—just as the maiden Jael did when she drove a tent peg through the temple of the enemy commander, Sisera (Judg. 4:22–23).

God's promise is that women will share in the victory. They will not just watch the battle from the sidelines; they will be actively involved in this spiritual conflict. So if you have been called into the Lord's army, don't give up if you feel you have been marginalized or mistreated. Many women have paid a higher price than you have, and their example can give you hope.

Hold on to the promises of God's Word, and pray for courage to break through the obstacles that stand in your way. And remember: Your enemy is Satan, not men, churches or denominations. Show nothing but love to the men (and women) who resist you, and bless those who misunderstand your calling. Trust God, who will open the door for you in His timing.

Notes

Introduction

1. Rebecca Price Janney, *Great Women in American History* (Camp Hill, PA: Horizon Books, 1996), 149.
2. Ibid., 149–150.
3. S. Lewis Johnson, "Role Distinctions in the Church," in Wayne Grudem and John Piper, eds. *Recovering Biblical Manhood and Womanhood* (Wheaton, IL: Crossway, 1991), 154.

Question #1
Forgiving the Men in Your Life

1. John Kie Vining, *When Home Is Where the Hurt Is* (Cleveland, TN: Family Ministries, n.d.), 64.
2. John Bevere, *The Bait of Satan* (Lake Mary, FL: Charisma House, 1994), 15.
3. R. T. Kendall, *Total Forgiveness* (Lake Mary, FL: Charisma House, 2002), 20–28.
4. Ibid., 3.

Question #2
Who's the Boss?

1. Catherine Clark Kroeger, "The Classical Concept of 'Head' as 'Source,'" (Appendix III) in Gretchen Gaebelein Hull, *Equal to Serve* (Grand Rapids, MI: Baker Books, 1998), 279–281.

Question #3
Men Behaving Badly

1. Carolyn Holderread Heggen, "Religious Beliefs and Abuse," in Catherine Clark Kroeger and James R. Beck, eds., *Women,*

Notes

Abuse and the Bible (Grand Rapids, MI: Baker Book House, 1996), 16–24.

2. Vining, *When Home Is Where the Hurt Is,* 78.
3. James M. and Phyllis Alsdurf, "A Pastoral Response," in Anne L. Horton and Judith A. Williamson, eds., *Abuse and Religion: When Praying Isn't Enough* (Lexington, MA: Lexington Books, 1988), 225–226.
4. Heggen, "Religious Beliefs and Abuse," in *Women, Abuse and the Bible,* 26.

Question #4
Married...With Children

1. John Wesley, *The Works of John Wesley* (Grand Rapids, MI: Zondervan, 1958), 1:386, quoted in Ruth Tucker and Walter Liefeld, *Daughters of the Church: Women and Ministry from New Testament Times to the Present* (Grand Rapids, MI: Zondervan, 1987), 238.
2. Ibid., 242.
3. Ibid., 238.
4. Catherine Booth, *Life and Death, Being Reports of Addresses Delivered in London* (London: Salvation Army, 1883), 11, quoted in Tucker and Liefeld, *Daughters of the Church,* 267.
7. Maria Woodworth-Etter, *A Diary of Signs and Wonders* (1916, reprint Tulsa, OK: Harrison House, 1981), 26.

Question #5
Diapers and Day Care

1. Hull, *Equal to Serve,* 161.
2. "Golda Meir: Women's Voices: Quotations by Women," Women's History, retrieved from the Internet at http://womenshistory.about.com/ library/qu/blqumeir.htm.

3. Thetus Tenney, "The Seasons of a Woman's Life," *SpiritLed Woman* (October/November 1998): 24.

Question #6
The Working Woman's Dilemma

1. "Women's History Month," *The Inventor's Museum,* retrieved from the Internet at www.inventorsmuseum.com.
2. Jackson Ekwugum, "10 Most Influential Christians in 2002," *Lifeway* (January/February 2003): 44–45.
3. *Transformations II: The Glory Spreads* (video), produced by George Otis Jr., The Sentinel Group, Seattle, Washington. Copyright © 2001.

Question #8
When Marriage and Ministry Collide

1. Edith L. Blumhofer, *Aimee Semple McPherson: Everybody's Sister* (Grand Rapids, MI: Eeerdman's, 1993), 77.
2. Ibid., 105.
3. Ibid.
4. Charles Trombley, *Who Said Women Can't Teach?* (South Plainfield, NJ: Bridge/Logos Publishers, 1985), 151.
5. Bob Sorge, *The Fire of Delayed Answers* (Canandiagua, NY: Oasis House, 1996), 60.

Question #9
Let's Hear It for Single Women

1. Martin Luther, quoted in Will Durant, *The Reformation: A History of European Civilization from Wycliffe to Calvin, 1300–1564* (New York: Simon and Schuster, 1957), 416, quoted in Tucker and Liefeld, *Daughters of the Church,* 173.
2. Linda Belleville, *Women Leaders and the Church* (Grand Rapids, MI: Baker Book House, 2000).

Notes

3. Billy Bruce, "When the Men Didn't Go, These Women Did," *Charisma* (December 2000): 52.
4. Ibid.

Question #10
Women Aren't Second String

1. Robert Speer, *Servants of the King* (New York: Interchurch, 1909), 144, quoted in Tucker and Liefeld, *Daughters of the Church*, 304.

Question #11
Role-Playing and Other Dumb Games

1. John Milton Williams, "Woman Suffrage," Bsac 50, April 1893, 343, in Carroll D. Osborn, ed., *Essays in Women in Earliest Christianity*, Vol. II (Joplin, MO: College Press, 1995), 461.
2. Ibid., 460.
3. "Women and the Industrial Revolution," *Watchman-Examiner* 8, no. 9 (February 26, 1920), in *Essays in Women in Earliest Christianity*, 461.

Question #12
Dare to Be a Pioneer

1. Hull, *Equal to Serve*, 141.
2. Gilbert Bilezikian, *Beyond Sex Roles* (Grand Rapids, MI: Baker Book House, 1985), 143–144.
3. For more information about Jackie Holland, read Carol Chapman Stertzer, "No Longer a Victim," *Charisma* (March 2001).
4. For more information about Danita Estrella, read Mary Hutchinson, "How One Woman Took Hope to Haiti," *Charisma* (July 2001).

5. For more information about Diane Dunne, read Peter K. Johnson, "New York's Homeless Pastor," *Charisma* (December 2002).

6. For more information about Suzette Hattingh, read Tomas Dixon, "She Dared to Claim a Continent," *Charisma* (October 2002).

7. For more information about Cathi Mooney, read Steve Lawson, "Reaching San Francisco's Deadheads," *Charisma* (April 2000).

Question #13
Strong Men, Weak Women

1. Philo, *Questions on Genesis,* Book I, 33, quoted in Tucker and Liefeld, *Daughters of the Church,* 63.

2. Plato, *Timaeus* 90e, quoted in "Greek Philosophy on the Inferiority of Women," retrieved from the Internet at, *The History Net,* www.womenhistory.com.

3. Ibid.

4. Plato, *Timaeus* 90e, quoted in Anne Dickason, "Anatomy and Destiny: The Role of Biology in Plato's View of Women," in Carol. C. Gould and Marx W. Wartofsky, eds., *Women and Philosophy* (New York: Putnam Publishing Group, 1976).

5. Trombley, *Who Said Women Can't Teach?,* 202.

6. Harold J. Chadwick and John Foxe, *The New Foxe's Book of Martyrs* (North Brunswick, NJ: Bridge-Logos Publishers, 1997), 344.

Question #14
What Do We Do With Deborah?

1. Katherine C. Bushnell, *God's Word to Women* (Mossville, IL: God's Word to Women Publishers, 1923), 286.

2. Grudem and Piper, eds., *Recovering Biblical Manhood and Womanhood,* 72.

Notes

3. Ibid., 216
4. Ibid.
5. Sue and Larry Richards, *Every Woman in the Bible* (Nashville: Thomas Nelson Publishers, 1999), 94.

Question #15
The Good Ol' Boys Club

1. Trombley, *Who Said Women Can't Teach?*, 34.

Question #16
Are Women Elders Called Elderettes?

1. Richard and Catherine Kroeger, *Women Elders: Called by God?* (Louisville, KY: Women's Ministry Unit, Presbyterian Church, U.S.A., 1980), 16.
2. John Chrysostom, *Commentary on Romans, Nicene and Postnicene Fathers,* First Series, XL, 555, quoted in Krueger, *Women Elders: Called by God?*, 17.
3. Kroeger, *Women Elders: Called by God?*
4. Ibid., 21. The Greek word used here is *hieroprepeis*, which can actually mean "to act like a priestess."
5. Ibid., 21.
6. Ibid., 18.
7. Ibid.

Question #17
Shhh! Be Quiet, Girls!

1. Walter C. Kaiser Jr., "Shared Leadership," *Christianity Today* (October 3, 1986): 124; Joseph H. Thayer, *Thayer's Greek-English Lexicon of the New Testament* (Nashville: Broadman Press, 1977), 275. AUTHOR'S NOTE: Scholars have long argued about the authenticity of 1 Corinthians 14:34–35 because the two verses have been moved around in various

versions. Some early manuscripts place the passage after verse 40; therefore, many scholars have theorized that the two verses in question were inserted later, after Paul's authorship, by a copyist. Theologian Gordon Fee, for example, argues that those who insist that Paul wrote these two verses have never been able to adequately explain why they were moved. It is the author's opinion that Paul inserted the passage because he was quoting from the letter he was answering.

2. Notes, *The New American Standard Study Bible,* Kenneth Barker, gen. ed., (Grand Rapids, MI: Zondervan, 1999), 1390.
3. Trombley, *Who Said Women Can't Teach,* 29
4. Ibid., 29–37
5. Ibid., p. 37

Question #18
It's All About Eve

1. Tucker and Liefeld, *Daughters of the Church,* 103.
2. Trombley, *Who Said Women Can't Teach?,* 203.
3. Ibid., 205.
4. Ibid., 202.
5. Ibid., 206.
6. Bilezikian, *Beyond Sex Roles,* 180.
7. Richard and Catherine Clark Kroeger, *I Suffer Not a Woman* (Grand Rapids, MI: Baker Book House, 1992), 99–113.
8. Loren Cunningham and David Hamilton, *Why Not Women?* (Seattle, WA: YWAM Publishing, 2000).

Question #19
Covered ... or Covered Up?

1. Helen Barrett Montgomery, *Western Women in Eastern Lands* (New York: Garland, 1987).

Notes

2. Grudem and Piper, eds., *Recovering Biblical Manhood and Womanhood.*
3. Tucker and Liefeld, *Daughters of the Church,* 301.
4. Ibid., 302.
5. Bilezikian, *Beyond Sex Roles,* 161.

Question #20
When Women Are in Charge

1. Janet and Geoff Benge, *Hudson Taylor* (Seattle, WA: YWAM Publishing, 1998), 17.
2. Earl O. Roe, ed., *The Henrietta Mears Story* (Ventura, CA: Regal, 1990).
3. Richard and Catherine Clark Kroeger, *I Suffer Not a Woman* (Grand Rapids, MI: Baker Book House, 1992), 87–98.
4. Ibid., 103.

Question #21
Whom Are You Calling Jezebel?

1. John Foxe, *Foxe's Christian Martyrs of the World* (Chicago: Moody, n.d.), 542–546.
2. Tucker and Liefeld, *Daughters of the Church,* 223.
3. 2001 Statistics, International Church of the Foursquare Gospel, retrieved from the Internet at www.foursquare.org.
4. Tucker and Liefeld, *Daughters of the Church,* 259.

Question #22
Pastors Who Wear Lipstick

1. Grudem and Piper, eds., *Recovering Biblical Manhood and Womanhood,* 72.

Question #23
The Stigma of Divorce

1. Craig Kenner, ...*And Marries Another* (Peabody, MA: Hendrickson Publishers, 1991), 88.
2. Ibid., 66.
3. Ken Walker, "The Scarlet Letter 'D,'" *Ministries Today* (March/April 1997): 40–41.

Question #24
Tough Choices

1. Carol Chapman Stertzer, "Angels in Afghanistan," *Charisma* (September 2002): 46.

Question #25
Don't Give Up on the Church

1. Ken Gill, "From Slave to Evangelist," in John D. Woodbridge, ed., *Ambassadors for Christ* (Chicago: Moody Press, 1994), 60–62.
2. *Amanda Smith: An Autobiography* (Chicago: Meyer and Brothers, 1893), 281, quoted in Tucker and Liefeld, *Daughters of the Church*, 271.
3. Ibid.
4. Ibid.
5. Harold Ivan Smith, "The Teacher Who Tamed the Klan," in Woodbridge, ed., *Ambassadors for Christ*, 87–88.
6. Maria Nilsen, *Malla Moe* (Chicago: Moody Press, 1956), 143, in Tucker and Liefeld, *Daughters of the Church*, 309.
7. Bushnell, *God's Word to Women*, 93.
8. Ed Silvoso, *Women: God's Secret Weapon* (Ventura, CA: Regal Books, 2001), 17.

Suggested Reading

Belleville, Linda L. *Women Leaders and the Church: 3 Crucial Questions.* Grand Rapids, MI: Baker Book House, 2000.

Bilezikian, Gilbert. *Beyond Sex Roles: What the Bible Says About a Woman's Place in Church and Family.* Grand Rapids, MI: Baker Book House, 1985.

Bristow, John Temple. *What Paul Really Said About Women.* San Francisco, CA: Harper San Francisco, 1991.

Bushnell, Katherine. *God's Word to Women.* Mossville, IL: God's Word to Women Publishers, 1923.

Cunningham, Loren, and David J. Hamilton. *Why Not Women? A Biblical Study of Women in Missions, Ministry and Leadership.* Seattle, WA: YWAM Publishing, 2000.

Grady, J. Lee. *10 Lies the Church Tells Women: How the Bible Has Been Misused to Keep Women in Spiritual Bondage.* Lake Mary, FL: Charisma House, 2001.

Groothuis, Rebecca Merrill. *Good News for Women.* Grand Rapids, MI: Baker Book House, 1997.

Hoppin, Ruth. *Priscilla's Letter: Finding the Author of the Epistle to the Hebrews.* N.p.: Lost Coast Press, 2000.

Hull, Gretchen Gaebelein. *Equal to Serve: Women and Men Working Together Revealing the Gospel.* Grand Rapids, MI: Baker Book House, 1987.

Jantz, Gregory L. *Healing the Scars of Emotional Abuse.* Grand Rapids, MI: Fleming H. Revell, 1995.

Keener, Craig S. *Paul, Women and Wives: Marriage and Women's Ministry in the Letters of Paul.* Peabody. MA: Hendrickson Publishers, 1992.

————. *... And Marries Another: Divorce and Remarriage in the Teaching of the New Testament.* Peabody, MA: Hendrickson Publishers, 1991.

Kroeger, Catherine Clark, and James R. Beck. *Women, Abuse and the Bible.* Grand Rapids, MI: Baker Book House, 1996.

Kroeger, Catherine Clark, and Al Miles. *Domestic Violence: What Every Pastor Needs to Know.* Minneapolis, MN: Fortress Press, 2000.

Kroeger, Catherine Clark, and Richard Clark Kroeger. *I Suffer Not a Woman: Rethinking 1 Timothy 2:11–15 in Light of Ancient Evidence.* Grand Rapids, MI: Baker Book House, 1992.

Silvoso, Ed. *Women: God's Secret Weapon.* Ventura, CA: Regal Books, 2001.

Trombley, Charles. *Who Said Women Can't Teach?* South Plainfield, NJ: Bridge-Logos Publishers, 1985.

Tucker, Ruth A., and Walter Liefeld. *Daughters of the Church: Women and Ministry from New Testament Times to the Present.* Grand Rapids, MI: Zondervan, 1987.